The Word of the Lord

Reflections on the ASB Readings

SUSAN SAYERS

Kevin Mayhew

First published in 1992 by
KEVIN MAYHEW LTD
Rattlesden
Bury St Edmunds
Suffolk IP30 0SZ

The Word of the Lord
is extracted from
Springboard to Worship

ISBN   0 86209 249 3

Cover design by Graham Johnstone
Typesetting and Page Creation by Anne Haskell
Printed and bound in Hong Kong.

Contents

Introduction

One of the ways we can prepare ourselves for communal worship each Sunday is by reading the chosen passages of scripture and reflecting over them prayerfully during the week. We can either do this alone, with a friend, or in small groups, and the whole worshipping community will be richer for this preparation of the Word.

The ideas and thoughts which are provided in this book are intended to start you thinking. It may be that just a word or sentence will help you begin to listen to what God is saying, both to you and your local church, and this may be teaching, encouragement, comfort, challenge or discipline. Please do not read these notes, then, as anything more than 'starters' – the real teaching will come as you spend time with God in prayer, expectant and receptive to him.

Begin your preparation with a time of stillness, focusing your attention and your love on Christ. Read through each scripture passage and its notes in turn, with time for discussion and reflection before going on to the next.

There may well be some things you don't immediately understand; having asked God to enlighten you, walk through the week consciously open to his teaching through events, people or situations you encounter. Jesus promised that whenever we seek, we will find, and we can trust him to keep his promise, however new, lost, jaded or guilty we may be feeling.

It is a good idea to keep a notebook handy, so that you can write down any fresh insights you are given and act on them.

Susan Sayers

9th Sunday before Christmas

God created our universe and everything in it, including us. He gives us both physical and spiritual life and sustains his creation with his constant love. As Lord of life he is worthy of all the praise, honour and worship that we can offer.

YEAR 1

GENESIS 1:1-3, 24-31A

Our world did not arrive by accident. The order which characterises the whole universe is not the result of a number of random coincidences and chance developments. The world has occurred because God wanted it to. This divine, creative life-force planned and willed it all to happen. The beautiful poem of creation in Genesis is written to express this fundamental truth, rather than formulate an exact scientific account of events. The finer details of order and method are far less important than the humbling realisation that some great and powerful being instigated all that we know and a good deal that we don't know. Lovingly it was brought into existence because God knew it was a good idea. He chose to create a you and a me. The world he has made is intrinsically good and fully in accordance with God's will.

COLOSSIANS 1:15-20

Paul is claiming for Jesus of Nazareth a far higher and greater identity than that of a good man, fine moral leader or outstanding prophet. To claim that he is actually the image of the unseen God is outrageous and challenging. Sometimes it seems easier to believe in God as a vast and cosmic power, the great Spirit of the Universe, the force of Love and source of Life, separate from the man of Galilee, healing, teaching and dying on a Roman gallows.

As soon as we recognise Jesus as being one with the all-powerful creative God – God with a human face – we are bound to listen intently to Jesus' teachings, follow him doggedly, talk to him and introduce him to our friends. If we are at all interested in our individual and collective purpose, we shall find answers to our questions in the reconciling life and death of Jesus, the Christ.

JOHN 1:1-14

Those who spent a lot of time with Jesus could see the divine glory in the grace and truth of this remarkable person. Jesus, the Word of God, is expressing God's character in his behaviour in Palestine just as he had expressed it at the very beginning of creation. Jesus is amazing proof that God loves us enough to get personally involved with us, without waiting for us to become worthy of such attention. Because of this there is always hope in every situation, which we can claim as soon as we claim Jesus Christ as Lord of our lives.

YEAR 2

GENESIS 2:4B-9, 15-END

This is the older of the two creation stories in Genesis, usually known as the J tradition because it refers to God as Jahweh, or Jehovah. In it we see man and woman working in partnership with God in the very rich and beautiful world he has made. There is a sense of comfortable companionship between these created beings and the Lord who has made them. Under God's authority they are able to enjoy the freedom of the garden, including the tree of life itself. It is only the usurping of God's authority – the challenging of his basic principles of good and evil – that is forbidden, for that is bound to fracture the fine tuning of God's world, disrupt the mutual trust he has created and damage the natural harmony that comes from living life in fellowship with him.

REVELATION 4

On earth we are surrounded by the evidence of God's glory, mastery, imagination, humour and order. Just as a close study of an artist's exhibition enables us to grasp something of the way he thinks and feels, so a walk through life provides us with plenty of glimpses into the nature of our creator.

In this vision John the Divine sees God's glory in a rare and startling directness. Obviously the sight is impossible to describe in earthly terms, but John expresses it in terms of purest light, brilliant as jewels, bright with a surrounding rainbow, charged with power like a thunder storm. We are given a wonderful sense of the creative force from which we and all things in heaven and earth spring; God is at the very centre of our universe and his majesty and power are truly awesome. He is no man-sized god, but the infinitely gracious Lord, worthy of all praise and honour.

JOHN 3:1-8

We are spiritual, as well as physical beings, created not just for seventy-odd years in this world but also for eternity. Often people become aware of their spiritual selves by virtue of neglect. There is a gnawing restlessness which refuses to be satisfied by the acquisition of material goods, busy lives or even close relationships, and never finds rest until it encounters the peace of God.

In his conversation with Nicodemus, Jesus explains that spiritual awakening as being born all over again. If we try to grasp spiritual truths entirely in physical terms then it will all seem, as it did to Nicodemus, very puzzling and incredible. But when we remember that God is Spirit, greater than time and space, infinitely present and personally involved with our lives, which he designed and is nurturing at this very moment, then we realise that to live completely the physical is inadequate; like trying to explore Africa by sitting in an armchair with an atlas.

8th Sunday before Christmas

The destructive nature of sin separates us from God through our disobedience to his will. It was God's love for us that prompted him to give his only Son so that we could be bought back, or redeemed, from the sentence of death and given the chance of new life in Christ.

YEAR 1

GENESIS 4:1-10

In this story we watch the resentment of Cain fester into hatred and then murder, as sin takes control of his life. From the beginning he was grudging. Abel had offered the best of his flock to God, while Cain offered only some of his produce from the soil. Typical of humankind, Cain found it bitter to delight in his brother's joy and success, and instead he allowed his resentment to feed a self-pitying grouse at the unfairness of life.

As soon as we allow sin to master us even in the smallest area of our lives, we increase our vulnerability and polish the slide for a rapid descent into evil. None of us is immune from the risk. None can assume it only happens to all the rest. Murder takes many forms, and though we may not commit it directly, God will expect us to accept responsibility for our fellow humans. If someone dies as a result of our self-indulgence or refusal to share the world's resources, or lack of interest in providing a fresh water supply for all earth's inhabitants, then we cannot try to excuse ourselves from being partly to blame.

I JOHN 3:9-18

In fact, if we do remain blind to the needs of our brothers and sisters, John says we are proving that we do not really love God, however much we claim to love him. True love is bound to show itself in the way we spend our time, talents and money, and in the way we behave, whether anyone we want to impress is watching us or not.

It would be so depressing to feel we had to struggle ineptly along the right path, knowing our habits and certain of failure. Fortunately, we don't have to. God promises to live within us and we couldn't get more constant and individual help than that!

Such help is vital. We need constant protection against temptation; we are also likely to be disliked, hated or even attacked, as Abel was, once people see our lives shining with Christian love. Bright shining shows up our own darkness.

MARK 7:14-23

That bad feeling inside comes out as spiteful words, or unkind behaviour, and no amount of ritual, or correctly followed rules, can take the place of genuine sorrow at sin committed and a longing to love God better.

The trouble is, we like making rules because then we can follow them and feel smugly that we have completed our duty. But God's values reach deep into the intentions behind our actions, the hidden resentments and secret refusals to forgive. We may fool other Christians with our empty observance of religious customs, but we do not fool God.

YEAR 2

GENESIS 3:1-15

See how subtle the stages of temptation can be. First the seeds of doubt are sown which cast a slur on God's motives in making his rules. Is it really for our own good that we are not to eat the fruit or indulge ourselves. Or is it perhaps God's way of keeping us in our place? At once the ambition to be totally powerful takes root, and we look for ways to justify what we have already decided to do.

The result of Adam and Eve's disobedience is to drive home to them just how naked and vulnerable they are. That is why they are suddenly frightened of God and hide from him.

ROMANS 7:7-13

Sin is always deceitful, often using what is intrinsically good to twist our priorities, misguide and coax us into behaving in ways which are contrary to God's law of Love. Paul found that even the Law itself had been used to tempt him into sin, by spelling out possible evil he hadn't thought about before. Similarly, news reports condemning certain actions may start a copycat reaction. The point is that while neither the Law nor the news reports are wrong, sin is devastatingly cunning, and we need to be constantly on our guard to avoid being tricked into it.

JOHN 3:13-21

If evil is so cleverly woven into the fabric of our existence, what chance can we possibly have of living good lives? Surely our weakness condemns us before we've even got started. Fortunately, evil is not the strongest force in the universe. God is utterly good, and loving enough to risk rejection by creating us with free will to choose right or wrong; loving enough to confine himself as man to save us from the mess of sin we get ourselves into.

Believing in Christ is a strong, unbreakable life-line that holds us firmly through temptation and rescues us whenever we feel ourselves slipping. The choice between using that life-line and foundering in sin is left to us.

7th Sunday before Christmas

Real faith is bound to be revealed in action. Abraham was prepared to trust God absolutely, even when he could not understand what he was being asked to do, and God honoured such faith. It is no good talking about having faith in God if we are not prepared to translate it into loving action and obedience to his will.

YEAR 1

GENESIS 12:1-9

Abram's obedience is so simply told that it sounds quite easy. In fact, it must have been a great upheaval and a move which was no doubt ridiculed as senseless by many. Why did he want to uproot everything and wander off, leaving all his security behind, for goodness' sake?

Obviously Abram was not like a reed in the wind, easily persuaded by anybody. So he must have recognised that this calling, though unusual and unexpected, was nonetheless full of authority. He sensed the greatness of God, and bowed before it, committing his future security and welfare to God's protection. If we say that we acknowledge God's greatness, then we must show it to be true in the way we willingly submit to changes, new directions, dangerous or unpleasant undertakings, without grumbling about what we have had to give up. Whenever we are called forward we shall have to leave something behind. But God will be going with us, so we shall end up not poorer, but richer.

ROMANS 4:13-END

Abraham is a shining example of faith, since he believed God's promise in spite of all its seeming impossibility. The practical details were left trustingly in God's capable hands because Abraham had no doubt about either God's power or his unswerving loyalty. It was this great faith which saved, or justified him, as it is our faith which speaks for us.

We may have to begin by wanting to believe, and asking for faith. We may be helped to it by being encouraged to step out, without support being visible, like a beginner on to an ice rink. Gradually we will be encouraged to take greater 'risks' trusting in God, instead of trusting in the more obvious support of our own strength, energy, intelligence or influence. That is not easy, especially if we prize our independence and resourcefulness. But it is essential if we are to learn to trust God. The fruit of that love will be increased love for one another.

JOHN 8:51-END

Sadly, some of those claiming most vehemently to trust God were unable to recognise him when he stood among them in the person of Jesus. Consequently their reaction to hints of his divinity ('before Abraham was born, I am') is such violent anger at his 'blasphemy' that they pick up stones to throw at him.

How was it possible for such a terrible misunderstanding to occur among those who studied God's law? Is it possible that we may act with similar blindness to Christ's presence in the world? For answer we are referred by Jesus back to Abraham once more. He, says Jesus, was overjoyed to see the Christ – God incarnate. His faith allowed him to 'see'. Where we rely only on proved, rational, visible evidence, we are effectively shutting out whole landscapes of insight which we might call Wisdom, or spiritual perception. This is the only way we can hope to stay in touch with God's truth, and it comes through living in his company.

YEAR 2

GENESIS 22:1-18

It must have seemed utterly incomprehensible to Abraham that God should ask him to sacrifice the very son through whom the promise of a chosen nation was to be fulfilled. If Isaac were killed, how could God's word possibly come true?

Perhaps Abraham was on the edge of trusting more in the means of achieving results than in the source of the power. Such a drastic threat to the 'means' threw Abraham's faith squarely on to the author of the promise. Since he was prepared to sacrifice even his beloved son, Abraham proved that even his most cherished hopes were second to his desire to serve God faithfully.

It was not any blood-sacrifice that God required. He needed Abraham to sacrifice 'faith-in-other-things', however closely those things may be tied up with his will. And it is all too easy to start trusting in the means instead of the source. If anything seems to be steering our attention away from God, we may find we are asked to abandon it, even though it is intrinsically good. Perhaps, once we have refocused our priorities, it will be given back abundantly; but by that time we will have sacrificed our faith in it, so our trust in God will have grown.

JAMES 2:14-24 (25,26)
James' sardonic humour drives the point home: faith without action is ridiculously ineffective. Our faith is dead and barren if we think our Christian duty is done by praying for the needs of the world on Sunday and sympathising from a safe distance.

God's idea of faith is rather different. He expects us to take an active part in helping those in need and changing what is wrong in society. A truly Christian community can never be apathetic or complacent. Christians should be positively involved in the community, not instead of church-going, but as the natural result of worshipping the God of Love.

LUKE 20:9-17
Perhaps the key to this parable is the motive behind the killing of the heir to the vineyard. The tenants figure that if

he is out of the way they will be able to own the vineyard themselves. Get rid of your faith in God and you can live as selfishly as you like.

There is another point, too. The people listening are horrified at what Jesus says the owner will do. For some the abuse of the prophets and the rejection of Christ is not deliberate evil but the result of an appalling blindness – a total inability to recognise Christ in everyday situations. We sometimes talk about the 'eye' of faith; that gift of discerning God in daily life is available for the asking, and we need to cultivate it so as to avoid the risk of persecuting and rejecting the very God we claim to worship.

6th Sunday before Christmas

God promises to save his people, and he can be trusted to keep his word. Moses had faith in God's promise to set his people free from slavery. Our faith in Jesus can set us free from the binding chains of sin. He will lead us and protect us from evil.

YEAR 1

EXODUS 3:7-15

The voice of God sounds full of confident enthusiasm for this escape plan. Having seen the problem and chosen the right time and the right leader, it is as if he can't wait to get started! In contrast, Moses is thoroughly dubious and sceptical. He feels utterly inadequate and unsuitable for the job, and is pretty sure the children of Israel won't accept him anyway.

Well, if he were working in his own strength he would indeed be inadequate and unsuitable – anyone would be. But God has called him, and whenever God asks us to do something, he always provides the strength, gifts and skills necessary.

In Moses' case, the first thing necessary is reassurance. God provides this by identifying himself as the God of Abraham, Isaac and Jacob. This reminds both Moses and the Israelites that God has shown himself to be faithful through many generations, and his promises can be trusted now as then.

HEBREWS 3:1-6

Through his faith and obedience Moses is a valuable and respected servant in the 'household' of God. All that he worked for and looked forward to was fulfilled in the coming of Christ, who is not another servant but the Son and heir. As Christians, then, we follow not only the guidelines of the Law but also the living pathway – Jesus himself.

JOHN 6:25-35

In this teaching, following the feeding of the 5,000, Jesus shows how he is indeed the promised Saviour, who provides our sustenance for eternal, spiritual life, just as bread provides us with temporary, physical sustenance. It may seem amazing to us that the people had just been fed miraculously, and many sick had been healed, yet they still clamoured for a sign.

Two very human characteristics are in evidence here. One is our desire for the spectacular. Amazing though the multiplying of bread and fishes was, it was not a grand conjuring trick prefaced with a roll of drums. Just Jesus quietly breaking the food up and the people finding they are getting enough to satisfy their hunger. The other is the way we are apt to idolise our heroes and heroines instead of following the direction of their eyes towards God. Moses had constantly reminded the people that it was God who had looked after them so well and here Jesus has to remind them again. But their great regard for one of God's servants is proving an obstacle in their acceptance of the very Saviour Moses foresaw. God often shows himself in ways we are not expecting. It is important that we recognise his presence.

YEAR 2

EXODUS 6:2-8

From Abraham, starting out in faith, the promise of God pulses through the generations and the significant events in this emerging nation. The covenant between God and his people is a solemn pledge, and God's faithfulness has proved constantly trustworthy. Now Moses, too, is given assurance of God's love and concern for his people and the promise of escape from slavery.

God did not just set the creation events in motion and then drift off, leaving us to get on with it; he is, and always has been, bound to his creation in love, like a parent to a child. The anguish of the starving and oppressed reaches his ears and evokes deep compassion just as much in our generation as in the time of Moses. His power is sufficient for us, now, as it proved to be for the children of Israel then.

HEBREWS 11:17-31

Some of the Jewish Christians for whom this letter was written no doubt missed the clearly defined rules of the law. The Christian way of love for God and one another, based on life in Christ, means that the right way forward cannot be precisely planned in advance. Rather, we have to learn the water's lesson of flowing – being willing to go along with God's will, however odd, difficult or impossible it may seem.

The writer gives a glowing list of examples of people who have been prepared to step out in faith like this, trusting and obeying God, even in the most dark and dangerous times. In every case their faith was honoured.

MARK 13:5-13

God honours our faith when we witness, by word and behaviour, to Christ's saving love. We are never promised a bed of roses, or immunity from conflict. Tragedies and world disasters will not suddenly vanish either. But because we are fixed firmly on the eternal rock of Christ, we need no longer be panic-stricken and despairing when they occur. Rather, God will use us in the mess of hatred, oppression and deceit, his Spirit speaking eloquently through our voices.

Nor does this only happen in the more dramatic arenas of war and persecution. We may be the only Christian available to witness to a member of the family, a friend going through a bad patch, a child at our school, a patient at our hospital or a colleague at the office.

5th Sunday before Christmas

There is a faithful remnant of God's people, through whom the Good News of God's power and willingness to save is spread to all nations. At every stage of the journey there is bound to be conflict between good and evil, and many will try to lead others astray. But we are to be prepared for this, so that, watchful and alert, we may remain faithful to our calling as followers of Christ.

YEAR 1

I KINGS 19:9-18

Elijah is dejected and fearful, doubting his vocation and threatened by his enemies. Following his superb witness to God in the astonishing and victorious challenge to the worshippers of Baal, Elisha seems to be experiencing the 'sagging' that sometimes comes after much energy and concentration have been used. Satan is ready to use such times of exhaustion to undermine our faith and cause us to collapse in a soggy mass of self-pity, doubt or self-indulgence.

But how tenderly God ministers to his loyal servant, Elijah! Expressing himself as a quiet stillness, he shows Elijah that whatever turmoil and aggression he may be living through, there is a fundamental core of peace which is unshakeable, since it is God himself. Having reassured him, God gives Elijah practical work to do, companionship (in the form of Elisha), and the knowledge that he is supported by a remnant of 7,000 people who have remained faithful to God. Confidence restored, Elijah is empowered to resume God's work.

ROMANS 11:13-24

It must have been painful to Paul that so many of his own race failed to accept Jesus Christ as the promised Messiah. He reminds the Christians in Rome of the great debt they owe to the Jewish people, through whom Jesus became incarnate. Typical of the way God brings resurrection out of evil, the rejection of Christ by his own people has opened up the way for non-Jews to be reconciled to God through Christ.

But this should never lead us to dismiss God's chosen race. Eventually, not only the faithful remnant but the whole people will be reunited to the 'root', and we can only wonder at what will happen then, when God's great, good plan is fully realised. For the moment, our task is to make sure that we remain faithful, so that we do not risk separation from the true 'olive' – a chosen people, rooted in God.

MATTHEW 24:37-44

Jesus' teaching about the second coming gives us ample warning, if we will listen. The trouble is, we are always inclined to think that disasters are things that will happen to other people and not to us. There is, too, the temptation to presume rather heavily on God's mercy, forgetting that he is also a God of justice, and our side of the covenant is very important. We tend to tell ourselves that there will be plenty of opportunity to prepare ourselves for death and the second coming of Christ later on – when the children are off our hands, for instance, or once the decorating is finished, or when the ironing is out of the way.

Jesus tells his disciples quite clearly that we will not know when the Son of Man comes until it is too late to start preparing. There is only one time when we can prepare to make sure we are counted among his faithful when he comes: that time is now.

YEAR 2

ISAIAH 10:20-23

Throughout the Old Testament we see God's people in their swings from fervour to backsliding, such a familiar pattern of human behaviour. We are so easily distracted from the route we have promised to follow, and so ready to put our trust in anything which is immediate and obviously powerful.

The prophet sees that eventually, on the day of the Lord, believers will trust unswervingly in the one true God. Since he is a God of piercing purity, righteousness and justice, his coming in glory is bound to bring a dramatic annihilation of all that is evil, corrupt or in any way contrary to his will and character. If we are to look with eagerness for his coming, then, we need to make sure that we are reconciled to God whenever we sin, so that we remain faithful to all the goodness and love he embodies.

ROMANS 9:19-28
Not that God is ever destructive. On the contrary he shows infinite mercy and patience with those who stubbornly renounce and disobey him, holding back his judgement to allow everyone the chance of turning back to him of their own accord. We are included in this great harvest, called personally to be sons and daughters of our heavenly Father, who knows what will make us eternally happy and at peace, and longs for us to allow him access, so that he can make such lasting happiness and peace a reality.

Many of us prefer being potters to pots, and will never relax in the hands of our potter long enough for him to form us as he wants to. If only we could grasp that he only plans to make us more fully and joyfully ourselves, perhaps we would not spend so much energy resisting the call to be committed and faithful followers of Christ.

MARK 13:14-23
As nearly 2,000 years have gone past since Jesus was born, it is sometimes tempting to assume that the end of the world is unlikely to happen for thousands of years, and we can dismiss the teaching of Christ about it as an understandable

misunderstanding, quite in keeping with the restrictions of being fully human as well as divine. Do we really believe it will happen at all, or is death our individual experience of the coming of Christ in glory?

Surely we ignore the warnings to be alert and watchful at our peril. It is already a lot nearer than in Jesus' time, and we would be fools to reject the possibility of it happening in our own lifetime. No doubt Mary was taken by surprise to find that the Messiah promised for generations was actually going to be born in less than a year. It was important that she kept herself ready so that when the time was right she was both available and receptive. We too need to keep ourselves prepared, with our minds and hearts open and receptive.

1st Sunday in Advent

We need to prepare ourselves right away so that we shall be ready and receptive when Christ comes again in glory at the end of time. The great hope of Israel has already been fulfilled in the first coming of Jesus, born as a baby. We look back to that with wonder. The enormous love it shows, highlights the supreme goodness and compassion of the God whose second coming we await.

YEAR 1

ISAIAH 52:7-10

Prophecies often refer to both an immediate and a wider, more far-reaching event at the same time. It is rather like looking at a landscape, where you can focus on the nearest hill or whole mountains on the horizon, but the landscape contains both.

Here the message of hope to the exiled Israelites concerns both the return to their ruined city of Jerusalem, and also the worldwide fulfilment of God's salvation at the end of time. For us, living in the last age (that is, since the life of Jesus Christ) the hope is just as comforting and thrilling. Good ultimately triumphs over evil; the coming of God's kingdom, for which we pray so often, is already in the process of becoming a reality. No one is excluded from the precious gift of God's saving and liberating love.

I THESSALONIANS 5:1-11

The early Christians clearly expected the Day of the Lord to take place within a very short time – they thought in terms of months rather than centuries. Dates and times had therefore become too important an issue, causing unnecessary anxiety. Paul puts things back in perspective by reminding the Thessalonians of the only definite fact: the Day will come as a surprise, not when we are expecting it.

So we cannot live recklessly until the last minute and then build our lives on Christ in a few scrambled seconds. Rather, we have to prepare now. As our companionship with Christ gradually floods us with serenity, joy and selfless love, our lives will witness to the reality of salvation. Others will be drawn to reconciliation with their creator, so that for them, too, the Day of the Lord becomes a Day of hope and accomplishment, rather than judgement and terror.

LUKE 21:25-33

Many of us do not like to think too much about the second coming of Christ, displaying all the power and glory of God. Even a casual study of our universe hints at such colossal size, force and energy that to think of its final moments, accompanied by the sight of its maker, is utterly terrifying.

Jesus prophesies that it will indeed be a time of appalling terror for the human race, with the physical order chaotic and the whole universe affected. Yet, amazingly, we are encouraged to stand upright and hold our heads high when all this takes place. It is not to be a time of fear but of great excitement and joyful anticipation, for it heralds the fulfilment of all the good that has been planned and cultivated throughout the whole history of the universe. All things are about to come to a glorious completion, where the will of a supreme and loving God is carried out in its entirety, and humankind can join with its creator in an eternal harmony. Whether we experience this from a standpoint of life or death will not matter. The event is of such cataclysmic magnitude that even the barrier of death will be brushed aside. We can all look forward to it with the thrill of hope, knowing that nothing at all can separate us from the love of God, and that love is eternal.

YEAR 2

ISAIAH 51:4-11

The prophet's vision – of the homecoming of God's people amid great rejoicing and relief, is no narrow, nationalistic pipe-dream. Certainly it includes the return of an exiled people to their ruined city of Jerusalem, but it is much more than this. Remarkably, it encompasses the idea of the whole world, with all nations, every coast and island, every part of God's creation, being gathered to take part in the greatest homecoming of all. In the fullness of time God will act with infinite power and glory so that his will is fully accomplished.

Running through the prophecy are the words of encouragement and tremendous hope: though the final times will be marked by devastating suffering and terror, God's deliverance lasts for ever and will not be affected by anything – even death. No-one seeking to live according to God's law of love need have anything to fear.

ROMANS 13:8-END

Paul explains how all the commandments are different, detailed ways of living the law of love. If we love someone, that will rule out any thought or action that would hurt them, so the entire law can be summed up in the command to love God and our neighbour. The very fact that it is a command, rather than a suggestion, points us towards the kind of loving that is required It is not something we can choose to do if we feel like it, or reserve for use with attractive neighbours only. God's law of love involves the will as well as the emotions, and often begins in earnest only at the point where liking stops!

Since we have no idea when Christ's second coming will take place, we need to submit our lives to God's law of love straight away. Advent is a good time to do a spiritual stock check and undertake some reordering of our time, ambitions and priorities.

MATTHEW 25:31-END

Having seen the behaviour of Jesus in the Gospels, we are directed to think of God in terms of deep, caring and healing love, infinite compassion and understanding, mercy and patience. All this is wonderfully true. But we have to be sure that in concentrating on God's compassion and mercy we do not neglect other qualities, also shown to us in Jesus, such as his zeal for truth, purity and goodness. His committed obedience to God's will and his dislike of hypocrisy. We need to trust God to forgive us but without presuming on his mercy, for he is utterly good and will never put up with evil, excusing it as an indulgent parent may spoil a child.

For God never pretends we have not sinned; he sees sin for what it is, coaxes us to repentance and then generously forgives. So when he comes in glory there is no way that anything evil or hypocritically smug will survive – the very fact that God is totally good is bound to result in the death of evil ultimately. One way or another it will be wiped out, and obviously it is better for that to happen through repentance and forgiveness now rather than inevitable judgement later.

2nd Sunday in Advent

God has gradually revealed himself to us through his Word in the Bible. The Old Testament is an unfolding of God's will in creating and leading his people into the way of truth and love. Jesus Christ, in the New Testament, is the fulfilment of all the hopes and prophecies, for in him God lives among his people in person.

YEAR 1

ISAIAH 55

In this prophecy we can see how God calls to us in our need, our thirst, our hunger. He is able to satisfy in a lasting and complete way, and his offer is freely available, so no-one is barred from applying. Neither will stocks run out; surely too good a bargain to miss. Yet often we ignore God's offer, and rush off to sample all kinds of inferior products which promise distraction, admiration or instant success, only to be let down and find that deep down we are still thirsty, restless, and unfulfilled.

When we do respond to his call, we shall find peace activating a desire to align our wills and desires increasingly to God's will. This in turn sets in motion the spreading of God's Good News to the jaded, anxious world. For this has been God's will from the start – that through the binding relationship of God with his people all nations will eventually be drawn to know him and experience his love, peace and joy.

2 TIMOTHY 3:14-4:5

Timothy is what we might call a 'cradle Christian'. Whereas the older generation had made their commitment to Christ as adults, he has been brought up in the Christian faith from childhood. If he can remain true to his early teaching, and use it as a pool of wisdom for the challenges of his missionary work, he will be richly prepared for effective witness in his ministry.

It is important that teaching programmes in our parishes and homes keep pace with the children's development, exploring and explaining the Good News in ways appropriate to their age and understanding. Often the rejection of the Church by teenagers and young adults is actually a very valid rejection of the simplistic and childish image of God they are still being given. We have only to think of the varied and often unsavoury crowds who gathered around Jesus to see that his message is drastically distorted if squashed into a narrow mould of the 'meek, mild and thoroughly nice' variety.

Like Timothy, those who have been reared in the church should have a wonderfully rich knowledge to draw on which can guide and help many in their spiritual journey.

JOHN 5:36B-END

Can it really be that a thorough, detailed knowledge of the scriptures could still leave us spiritually blind? Surely the more knowledgeable we are about our Bible, the better Christians we must be.

Here Jesus explains the dreadful irony that it is indeed possible to scrutinise the scriptures for what we want to find, rather than what God wants to show us. And if this happens we shall fail to recognise the voice of Jesus, either through our Bible reading or in our lives and relationships, just as the scribes and pharisees failed to recognise in this preacher and healer from Nazareth the Messiah described and foretold by Moses and the prophets.

How, then, can we make sure that we do not fall into the same trap? Fortunately it has nothing to do with our I.Q., our status or our qualifications; all that is needed is to want to know and love God more. Everything else will be taken care of by God himself, who leads us by the best route for each one of us to a deeper understanding of his will, his personality and his plans for the world.

YEAR 2

ISAIAH 64:1-7

There are times when all of us, faced with blatant injustice or flagrant disregard for God's law of love, feel the surge of frustrated zeal for things to be put right once and for all, with God's power so dramatically obvious that the enemies of good will finally be knocked into sensing their need for repentance. James and John felt it too, when the Samaritan village wouldn't receive their master, and they were all ready to call down righteous fire from heaven to consume the whole lot of them, there and then.

But Jesus' reaction is to rebuke James and John, and set off to find another village. And the prophet in this reading also works through the understandable desire for immediate judgement. He recognises that those who trust God see him acting dramatically in their lives all the time; that it is our own individual lack of response to God that cuts us off from him, blows us like dead leaves further and further away from his presence; that if we have turned our faces resolutely away from God we shall not be able to escape the insidious distortion of our lives by slavery to the ugly master of sin.

The last line of the reading shows the prophet turning to God with all the trust of a young child: in spite of all our doubts and violent feelings, in spite of all our sin and weakness, we can turn to God as to a loving parent who knows and understands us.

ROMANS 15:4-13

The scriptures can direct us to a better grasp of this relationship, if we go to them with an open, receptive mind. Through them we will hear God, speaking through psalms and prophecies and through the history of the people of Israel. We will see God acting in the person of Jesus in many varied encounters with all kinds of people and problems. All of which will fill us with a hope which the world finds strange since it is independent of comfort and luck. And if such hope makes people envious, that may be their first step to acquiring it for themselves.

LUKE 4:14-21

Jesus is, at this point, popular with everyone and beginning to be famous. He chooses to travel back to his home town and announces that the words of Isaiah are being fulfilled right in front of them. Constantly throughout his ministry Jesus directed the people to see his works and teaching as the fulfilment of scripture, and never as isolated or rootless acts of spectacle. Those who were receptive could begin to grasp the startling truth that the promised Messiah was among them, even if he was different from what they had expected. Never was anyone whipped up by emotional pressure to accept this. Instead they were always given clear evidence that complied with God's revelation through scripture, so they could come to believe in him, just as we can, by reading the scriptures and assessing Jesus' 'good fruit'. Anyone merely out to see a miracle show was and is likely to be disappointed.

3rd Sunday in Advent

Be prepared for the coming of the Lord. John the Baptist was the promised forerunner to Christ, and his teaching inspired many to turn back to God's ways, making them receptive when Jesus began his ministry. We, too, need to renounce sin and prepare for the time when Christ will come again in glory.

YEAR 1

ISAIAH 40:1-11

Although the terrain is far from promising, and much has to be done before the highway can be constructed, the overriding message here is of great joy. The people are given comfort and consolation. This is because turning towards God and away from sin has put them in a right relationship with their creator, and all the hard work will now be positive: they will be working with God instead of against him.

We have only to look at the way people throw themselves into the preparations for a street party, carnival or Christmas decorating to see how eagerly we work for something special and exciting. This is the spirit in which we are urged to prepare ourselves for the Lord. Having faced up to sinfulness, having apologised to God for it and resolved to make amends, we can enjoy the hard work; enjoy getting our hands dirty by physical involvement in his service, and be happy that we are tired at the end of the day. We can get excited about the highway we are building and delight in the fellowship we share with all the other road workers.

When it is finished, the dazzling glory of our God will be revealed so that everyone can see it. That is well worth a few blisters and bruises.

I CORINTHIANS 4:1-5

As we work, we need to remember that we are not, so to speak, self-employed. The highway we build is not a sweeping driveway to our own private residence, yet it is a temptation sometimes to behave as if it were. As soon as we begin to work for ourselves instead of God's glory the spirit of criticism and judgement creeps in which drastically reduces the efficiency of the building programme. Paul urges us to leave all judgement of people to God, who is more than capable and has a perfect sense of timing. If we put all our energies into working as trustworthy servants and stewards of our Lord and Master, then his kingdom will be painstakingly established.

JOHN 1:19-28

In this account of John the Baptist's witness we see the heralding of the long-awaited Messiah, in images the people – with their sound knowledge of the prophets – would be likely to understand. John was fulfilling a role that was essential in preparing the way for Israel's Saviour. It would alert many to look for signs of God visiting his people, and guide them to see his presence where they may not have been expecting to find it.

If we join the crowds around John and wholeheartedly repent of all that is evil, ugly and damaging in our characters, we too shall be alerted to recognise Christ and see him more clearly.

YEAR 2

MALACHI 3:1-5

Malachi, speaking to a jaded and disillusioned society, where both moral and religious principles had become badly frayed, looks forward longingly to the Day of the Lord. Although his coming is bound to be caustic and stringent, it will bring about purity and integrity: reconciliation of the people with their God.

John the Baptist is foretold as the messenger who will clear a path in people's hearts so they are receptive and expectant when the Lord comes. For with us, as with them, a path needs to be prepared before we are able to welcome the Christ into our lives. He will remain standing outside our hearts, knocking, until we invite him in.

PHILIPPIANS 4:4-9

Here, in the full light of the coming of the Son of God into the world, Paul speaks with firsthand experience of the new, purified life rooted in God's love. It is a life radiant with joy, fulfilled and peaceful, constructive and purposeful, encouraging and thankful. And it is not just reserved for a few stained-glass or plaster saints. It is available for us in our world, complete with its violence, work pressures, materialism and corruption – a world in some ways quite similar to the one inhabited by these Philippians.

Certainly we are still journeying forward to the accomplishment of all things at the end of time, but through living in Christ's love the journey itself is part of the accomplishment of God's good plans for us, rather as, on a pilgrimage, the fellowship and expectancy of the travelling is an integral part of the arrival.

MATTHEW 11:2-15

The Old Testament has been a gradual unfolding of God's character and purpose, and there had been plenty of time for people to form fairly rigid ideas of the Messiah they were expecting.

John the Baptist's preparation of the people had been based on the awesome justice of the Messiah, who would sort out the good from the bad. So, in the harsh and depressing surroundings of Herod's prison, we find John perplexed and surprised at the way Jesus is behaving, wondering, even, if he might have been mistaken in thinking Jesus to be the promised Messiah.

We often find that God works through the most unlikely people and places, and must be on our guard against rejecting his presence because it is not where we expected to find it.

Jesus sets John's mind at rest by pointing to his own 'good fruit' in words described by the prophet in the book of Isaiah that John would have known so well. If the sick are healed, and the blind are given sight, then the evidence is there – God's saving love is at work. We have to make up our own minds as to whether or not we accept the evidence.

4th Sunday in Advent

*Mary was chosen by God to be the mother of Jesus, our Saviour.
God's great sign of love is that he is carried through a human
pregnancy and born into a human family which is descended
from David. In this way the prophecies are fulfilled and God's
glory revealed to the whole world.*

YEAR 1

ISAIAH 11:1-9

This remarkable prophecy recognises God's capacity for
achieving the seemingly impossible. The prophet looks
forward to a fundamentally changed world, free from
injustice and free from aggression, even in nature. Just as
strong, fresh shoots spring from tree stumps, so God's
promised Saviour will appear to transform and renew. And
the more we make ourselves right with God, enabling his
kingdom to be established in us, the closer our world will
become to a God-filled kingdom of peace and love.

I CORINTHIANS 1:26-END

Of course, there is often a huge contrast between Isaiah's
vision and the actual world. We, as well as the Corinthians,
live in a world which idolises and values the rich and
glamorous, and is far more ready to admire someone for
intelligence or beauty than compassion or integrity.

But God sees people so differently; to him it is the heart
– the inner core – of each person which is important and
lovable, and though some may also be rich, famous,
handsome or intelligent, these are not the qualities which
necessarily draw us closer to our fulfilment in Christ. In fact,
he often seems to choose fairly low-attainers on the worldly
list and then live so powerfully through them that the world
is eventually alerted. Paul himself was no oil painting. Saint

Francis was noted for looking so insignificant until he started preaching. In our own time, the world has started to seek out Mother Teresa, while she has never courted the world. And then there is even you and me! If we let him shine in us, he will certainly shine.

LUKE 1:26-38A

One in whom the shining grew to be God's Son was Mary. Her ready response teaches us how to react to God's calling in our own lives; it is so important to keep ourselves available, so that when God needs us we are ready. No one person is individually responsible for the success or failure of spreading God's kingdom, but God's great sense of order and timing can be aided or hindered by the individual's response.

For in this gentle and tender moment of the Annunciation, we are witnessing the convergence of many events, many lives and many spiritual journeys. They all merge at this particular point in time to enable the next great stage of God's salvation to be accomplished. And it all depends on Mary's response.

YEAR 2

ZECHARIAH 2:10-END

Reading prophecy is like looking out over a landscape. The view consists of both foreground and distance. We can focus on either, but in either case the complete view stays in sight. Many prophecies have both immediate and long-term significance, and both are important visions of God's truth. Certainly Zechariah is writing of the immediate and localised return of the Lord to Jerusalem. He also writes of a time which we, through reading the gospels, have all witnessed: the coming of God's Son to live among his people and direct them by his words and example to the loving nature of the Godhead. We are living in a time during which many nations are coming over to the Lord, and are co-workers with Christ in spreading God's kingdom.

REVELATION 21:1-7

The ultimate end of all this is the perfect completion of God's good plan for the universe he has created. That is seen here as the new Jerusalem, which represents the entirely new order of God's kingdom, lifting our imaginations beyond the material world as we know it until in the description we can sense something of the incredibly pure and glorious life possible when the whole of humanity is entirely at one with the loving creator.

Advent is a great celebration of hope, which sweeps us joyfully, triumphantly and yet humbly towards the straw-filled manger at Bethlehem.

MATTHEW 1:18-23

Nothing of this can ever take place without the willing consent of the people created by God. Now, as the world is poised before the Incarnation, we can watch with thankfulness as both Mary and Joseph allow their lives to be used by God. They are prepared to lay aside their own plans and hopes because God asked them to. Such acceptance and unselfishness can never be dredged from any of us for an important occasion unless we have trained ourselves by making many daily acts of unselfishness. Though none of these may make the headlines, the gradual tuning of ourselves to the Christ-way of living will enable us to be in top condition when we are asked to respond in a Christlike way at times of great importance. If we are available, then God can use us; if not, we actively obstruct his will.

Christmas Day

Christ, our Saviour, is born. Eternal God breaks into human existence to transform and redeem it. In the darkness of night, God's majestic glory becomes a vulnerable newborn baby. Creator of all is entirely dependent on those he has created. Such is the measure of his infinite love.

YEARS 1 AND 2

ISAIAH 9:2, 6-7

This great prophecy of healing and restoration is fulfilled in the incarnation. Nothing can disperse darkness but light, and now that light has come in the universal sign of hope – a new baby. With Christ being born, hope springs up, for the darkness can never win or overcome us any more. No wonder it is an occasion for rapturous delight and gladness – nothing can ever be quite the same again.

or

ISAIAH 62:10-12

There is such jubilation and relief in this fanfare of welcome. At last, with the coming of the Lord, all things shall be well. In a rush of enthusiasm and excitement God's people are urged to clear the way for a new era of love and justice. Now, as God, unannounced except by angels, slips into the middle of human life, we can join in the exultant joy of all heaven – for the promised Saviour has just been born.

or

MICAH 5:2-4

Faith seems easier to manage when there is rational, concrete evidence to support what we believe. Yet, in fact, real faith is only begun when that evidence is missing. Like Peter, we often start sinking at the thought because it makes us feel desperately vulnerable. It was during the blackest times of exile that the prophets remained convinced of God's promise to come and save.

Micah, seeing beyond the fallibility of human rulers, however noble, looks forward to the time when the Prince of Peace will rule over the whole land in a reign of unparalleled integrity and majesty, founded on the majesty of God himself. Like the great king David, he will hail from the insignificant town of Bethlehem, and the fact of his coming is not in doubt, however hopeless the immediate situation appears.

TITUS 2:11-14; 3:3-7
No one is let out of this message of salvation; Christ loves every individual in the entire human race, and longs for each one of us to be reconciled to our Father in heaven and to each other, as brothers and sisters in one close-knit family.

Christmas, with all its hope and happiness, is a wonderful opportunity to deepen bonds of love, offer reconciliation where there has been coldness or hostility, and push back the frontiers of our caring a little more, to include a wider circle of 'brothers and sisters'.

or

HEBREWS 1:1-5 (6-12)
Even before the swirling gases of our solar system were formed, God was fully present and active. It is well worth star-gazing, sometimes, to remind ourselves of the vastness of the universe and the immensity of God who had no beginning and will have no end. For that is the power which broke into a particular point in history by being born of a human woman at Bethlehem.

All through the world's development and birth pangs, all through the developing consciousness of humanity, and all through the visions and prophecies of perceptive, prayerful people, God was revealed. But never so clearly as when he lay in Mary's arms as the first-born baby in a human family.

or

I JOHN 4:7-14

Simply, yet profoundly, John explains the mystery of the incarnation in terms of God's immeasurable love for us. We do not have to grind ourselves to shreds trying to make ourselves worth saving. Neither can we save ourselves, however determinedly we may grit our teeth and try. Rather, we need to take a deep breath, relinquish our desire for independence from God and accept the caring love he has for us.

Once we grasp the extent of his love for us, loving care will spill out of us to others and result in some kind of ministry. But because it now grows out of our relationship with Christ, our attitude will be different, less frantic and more lighthearted; less grudging and more generous.

LUKE 2:1-14 (15-20)

The first reaction of the shepherds to seeing their familiar hillside filled with glory, is absolute terror. Faced with such awesome and naked power, they recognise their own weakness and vulnerability. Once the angels have reassured them, their amazement at God's power turns into ecstatic joy at the love such a powerful God must have if he is prepared to put aside that glory in order to save the creatures he has made.

Sometimes a glimpse of God's majesty stuns us and may scare us. We may feel tempted to argue it away, so that we can stay in our familiar territory. Many back away from the real God of glory because he is unpredictable and disturbing. They prefer their own, controllable, watered-down version.

But the one, omnipotent God is not only powerful, he is also a God of tenderness and compassion, and if we listen, we will always hear him reassure us whenever he challenges.

or

LUKE 2:8-20
Cataclysmic though the event of the incarnation was, it was
worked out in terms of inns and travellers, stables and
shepherds – just the ordinary, everyday things among
unremarkable people. It was as if God let himself in by a side
door, quietly and unobtrusively, just as he often does to many
hearts in every generation.

But once we find him there, the pleasure and excited
gladness of what his presence means opens our lives to a
richness we can hardly believe, and, like the angels and
shepherds, there is great rejoicing.

or

JOHN 1:1-14
Here the full expression of God shines out, as the Word
becomes flesh. The incarnation is an impossibility come true;
we wonder at the enormity of it, delight in the beauty of it
and perhaps balk at the courage of it. Can it really be possible
that the creative force behind every galaxy, every bacterium
and life itself, is actually here, with the name of Jesus,
walking about healing, teaching and listening to us? Yes, says
John, incredible though it seems, it is true, because we saw
his glory and it was the glory of God himself.

If we, also, are convinced by our experience of Jesus that
he really is God, we are bound to accept his teaching and
open our hearts to his love. And he will not only make us his
disciples, but also his sisters and brothers, all sharing God as
our loving Father.

1st Sunday after Christmas

We can see the great love of God personally in Jesus, the Christ. All the promises and hopes are fulfilled by the birth of this baby in Bethlehem, because he is the one who can set us free from our slavery to all that is evil. His salvation, beginning in Israel, extends outwards to include every created person.

YEAR 1

ISAIAH 7:10-14

In the face of a crisis, Ahaz is shaking like a leaf, and Isaiah tells him that such terror suggests he doesn't really trust in God. As an act of faith he is urged to ask God for a sign, but Ahaz prefers not to stick his neck out. He excuses his lack of faith by arguing that you shouldn't put God to the test anyway.

God's response is the affirmation that a new royal child of his own making will be established to put things in order and rectify the wrongs of weak and sinful humanity. With the birth of Jesus, this prophecy is to be stunningly fulfilled at nothing less than the cost of God's own Son.

God is supremely trustworthy; even in times of crisis and panic his power and faithfulness stand like rock. We need not be afraid for he is with us.

GALATIANS 4:1-7

Often Paul draws our attention to God's remarkably perfect sense of timing. In this letter to the Galatians we are helped to see how God, the Lord of eternity and time, holds and guides his creation in a perfectly ordered and finely balanced movement towards fulfilment and accomplishment. Like an heir waiting to come of age God's people lived expectantly. At the best and right time (both spiritually and historically) God works from within the Law to buy us a greater freedom than the Law could ever give.

JOHN 1:14-18

How do we know that all this was fulfilled in the person of Jesus of Nazareth? What was it about this man which convinced people they were in the presence of something greater than a fine teacher or clever miracle worker?

The two remarkable qualities which most impressed Jesus' disciples were not his power, his intelligence or his looks, but his grace and his truth. It is worth remembering these words to mull over whenever we have the opportunity, because they draw us closer to the character of God. These are the responsive, compassionate, vibrant qualities from which all Jesus' teaching and healing sprang. These are the personal characteristics of a loving and utterly pure God, which could not be revealed through the Law alone, but needed to be expressed through a living person.

YEAR 2

I SAMUEL 1:20-END

Hannah had longed desperately for a child, so now, when she keeps her vow to lend Samuel to the Lord as soon as he is weaned, we can appreciate the very great offering she is making. Sacrifice is always a costly gift; giving from the surplus of our possessions is not really a sacrifice at all. But neither is a costly gift given grudgingly or resentfully. Here, in Hannah's offering of her son to the Lord, we see a beautiful example of real sacrifice: the gift is very precious to her but is given lovingly and thankfully.

As a result of this Israel was provided with one of her finest spiritual leaders.

ROMANS 12:1-8

It is this same attitude to giving that Paul urges us to have: a generous-hearted giving back to God of our whole selves, complete with our gifts and talents, our time, our ambitions and our wills. That kind of giving digs rather deeper than most of us would wish! What about our right to self-fulfilment, our independent thinking, our earning potential and our leisure activities? Surely Paul isn't suggesting these should be disrupted or abandoned?

These questions, rushing to the surface in the face of such an all-inclusive challenge, highlight the differences between God's 'pattern' for living and the pattern of this present world, which emphasises the right to happiness and self-fulfilment and self-possession far more than the value of giving till it hurts.

Yet the strange truth is that in lovingly relinquishing our grip on all that in worldly terms makes for happiness, we find a deep-seated joy and fulfilment which is otherwise temporary.

LUKE 2:22-40
Both Simeon and Anna had abandoned their lives to God. They must have been in constant touch with him and were therefore ready to recognise, among the daily routines of the temple, the promised Saviour, though he was only a baby.

In this small child they perceived the fulfilment of ancient prophecies, both pain and victory. Joseph and Mary were given the incredible task of nurturing God's Son. God chose a family which was not famous, wealthy or well-connected. The best upbringing for God's Son was a home where he was loved and cherished, teased and laughed with.

So we need not worry about how our children are losing out if we cannot afford the latest toys or clothes. If we concentrate on the values God chose for his own Son we shall be giving our children the best possible start in life.

2nd Sunday after Christmas

God's Son, Jesus, shared with us all the experience of childhood. He grew up in a family which had its share of troubles as well as joys, and his love can fill our family life if we invite him to live among us in our homes.

YEAR 1

ECCLESIASTICUS 3:2-7

Here we find the practical love which Jesus taught and showed. It is so much easier to talk about love than to tend patiently to an irritating child, or repeat the same pieces of news time after time to an elderly relative whose memory is failing. Somehow, this mundane, everyday loving is especially difficult and demanding.

Yet from these threads the strong fabric of real love is woven. Perhaps if we think of them as opportunities, instead of frustrating time-wasters, we may find them easier to cope with, and even start enjoying the challenge!

or

EXODUS 12:21-27

We all have family jokes and traditions. They reinforce our sense of belonging. Through looking at the old family photograph albums, too, children learn about the special group they belong to, including those who may have died but are still remembered with affection.

In today's reading we see the family traditions of the Israelites being fixed in the minds of the people so that each new generation will celebrate the Lord passing over their houses and sparing them. The ritual keeps the memory alive and also prompts the curious young to ask 'Why?' If we go to church each Sunday, sooner or later our children will ask us why we do. We should never evade, suspecting mutiny! God has planned with this in mind; he gives us here an opportunity to tell them about his love.

ROMANS 8:11-17

'Abba' is much nearer to the meaning of 'Daddy' than 'Father', so it throws us into the relationship of a young, trusting child with a loving parent. It speaks of dependence, comfort, discipline, belonging and binding love. No longer struggling on our own to uphold moral standards, we are freed from so much pressure and stress. We do not have to carry the world's problems on our shoulders. Those fears are of the past: in the present we belong to God. His patience, his forgiving nature, and his willingness to show mercy are all there at our disposal to use liberally in all our relationships.

LUKE 2:41-END

Jesus' childhood was certainly not without problems. He was born away from home and the family were probably refugees until he was a toddler. When they did get back to Nazareth, no doubt some of the villagers would have gossiped about them. Luke's account of Jesus at twelve years old being left behind, his parents searching for him, desperately worried, gives us a glimpse of other special difficulties there may well have been in nurturing a child who was also God.

So it is not an absence of problems which marks out a Christian family from others. It is the way such problems are met; offered in love to God the everlasting Father, accepted and used as an opportunity for growth in patience, unselfishness or compassion.

YEAR 2

ISAIAH 60:1-6

Israel is to be the focus of the most astounding event of history. Through all her wanderings, escapes, defeat and exile, she has waited. God has kept by her, encouraged, chided and forgiven her, but still the long-term promise has yet to be fulfilled.

Now the prophet sings with the thrill of conviction and hope, of Israel being the centre of God's revelation: like a pulsing light glowing in the surrounding darkness, God's glory will attract all peoples, and the light will eventually flood the whole world.

It is a remarkable privilege, which excites national pride and awe-filled humility.

REVELATION 21:22-22:5

That prophecy came true in the person of Jesus. With him the new age begins; but it is not yet complete. We know this each time we open a newspaper and read of the violence, undeserved cruelty, the greed and the hatred which still run free in our world. We know it in ourselves whenever we sin against God and against each other. No one can pretend that evil was eradicated at the crucifixion.

This prophecy is a vision of the accomplishment of all the good that Jesus made possible by his life and death and resurrection. Slowly we edge towards it, both in our individual pilgrimage and as a species. All the good any one person does, hastens the coming of this kingdom; every loving act and word brings it closer; each time we forgive and promote peace we work with Christ in establishing heaven on earth.

MATTHEW 2:1-12, 19-23

Even as a tiny child, Jesus begins his work of drawing people to worship God. Here we see him with Mary and Joseph in Bethlehem, being honoured and presented with gifts from these important and mysterious strangers. They have been drawn by signs and promises to pay their respects, for they sense that in Jesus the light of the world has been born.

The Epiphany of our Lord

Wise men from distant countries were led to worship Jesus. The light of the living Christ also leads us, and when our lives reflect his light, many others will be drawn to worship the true God who made us and loves us.

YEARS 1 AND 2

ISAIAH 49:1-6

This reading is one of the so-called 'Servant' poems. It describes a figure who, in the role of God's servant, is commissioned to bring God's people back to him. At times the servant appears to be the people of Israel, who, through their covenant with God, are to be the means of bringing all other nations to worship their creator. At other times the servant seems to be an individual, who, through his example and suffering, will draw many to acknowledge and worship God. It may well be that both meanings are intended, and for us Christians the passage certainly sounds remarkably like the mission of Christ himself.

The important thing is that through his prophet God teaches that his salvation is not just for the people of Israel, but will, through them, flood through the entire world until every scrap of creation is filled with the knowledge of his saving love.

EPHESIANS 3:1-12

Paul acts as an ambassador. As a Jew, he fulfills Jewish prophecy by reaching out into the world's darkness with the light of God's saving love. God's truth had taken quite a time to dawn on Paul, and the dawning had been traumatic. But once enlightened, he worked fervently to spread the news.

Perhaps it has taken us years to realise that Jesus really is the Son of God, and that if we can bring ourselves to 'fall back on him' he does not let us drop. Perhaps a relative or friend has drifted away and seems to be taking anxious years to return.

It is important to remember that it is never too late to bother. However old we are, we can work wholeheartedly, for youth is not a prerequisite for being a full-blooded Christian. Also, some wanderings may be necessary for growth in some people's spiritual development and, if constant prayer is offered for their return to faith, they may well come back stronger and more receptive.

What we must never do is give up on them, even secretly. God never does that and neither must we.

MATTHEW 2:1-12
There are various possible explanations for the great bright light that led these enigmatic strangers to a small child living in Bethlehem. Whoever they were and wherever they travelled from, they knew they had arrived when they saw Christ. Here the searching stopped and the worshipping began. The focus of their lives was readjusted and they responded by giving.

Jesus, when he grew up, promised that everyone who searches will find. Sometimes people fool themselves into thinking that they are searching when really they have their hands over their eyes! Thorough searching involves setting out on a risky journey, asking directions from the scriptures and from those who have studied them, and being prepared for the star being occasionally hidden from view.

Do we provide enough help to those who are struggling through their search? Do we offer accommodation and hospitality on the way? Are we too ignorant of scripture to be able to answer their questions? Perhaps we could do more to guide them towards their destination.

1st Sunday after the Epiphany

Jesus is anointed at his baptism with the Holy Spirit. When we are baptised we are born again into new and lasting life. We are then given the power and all necessary ingredients for witnessing to God's love wherever he sends us. Together we work towards his kingdom which is founded on caring love.

YEAR 1

I SAMUEL 16:1-13A

The choice of this king was crucial and God had a particular person in mind for the job. But whether or not his will would be done depended on Samuel's readiness to comply with God's instructions even if that meant waiving his independent judgement. Fortunately Samuel stayed close to God and refused to anoint anyone until he felt God's firm assurance that this was the right man.

If we ever find that setbacks make it impossible to achieve some work we know God desires to have done, we must not make a bodged job with what seems to be available. We must wait and pray for clear guidance – the proper solution may be somewhere else, quite unexpected. The important thing is to stay listening, as God will show his way forward soon enough. Also, outward appearances count for little in God's eyes. He often rejects and chooses in ways which take us by surprise. Perhaps we should think twice before judging by appearances!

ACTS 10:34-38A

Peter is a firsthand witness to the remarkable ministry of Jesus which began in full after God had anointed him with the Spirit and with power at his baptism. As Peter now sees, it all began with a chosen few, but it is God's will that through them the news may be spread far and wide. The promise to forgive sins and set people free is there for everyone.

MATTHEW 3:13-END

How obedient Jesus was to the religious Law and customs! He, after all, had no need to be washed of sin, for he was sinless, so why did he insist on John baptising him?

In Jesus, God showed his desire to be completely identified with the creatures he had made. Now, at the point of baptism, he again shows full identification with the people; he is not above us but alongside us; in our sin and repentance as well as our odd moments of sanctity.

He also needed to be seen to be anointed by God, just as David had been anointed by Samuel. This expressed God's setting apart of someone for a special task. As Jesus came up from the water, God expressed his confirmation of love and power, both for Jesus himself, and for those whose spiritual eyes were open to understand.

YEAR 2

ISAIAH 42:1-7

The prophet must have been very close to the mind of God, for the character of the chosen servant he describes is remarkable in its capacity for mercy, compassion and lack of vengeance, in contrast to the climate of the time.

Jesus, having studied this passage from childhood, began to see how he must indeed be the fulfilment of this prophecy. All holy men and women share this ability to understand the divine character in some way which is nothing to do with knowing facts about him, or observing rules and rituals. Their understanding grows like a plant that is rooted in him; by keeping constantly in his company through prayer and meditation, they 'soak up' his essence, and it shows. He has invited us to this close companionship. If we accept, he will transform us in the same way, however unpromising the material!

EPHESIANS 2:1-10

We know only too well our tendency as humans to be self-centred and self-indulgent. Advertisers rely on it heavily for their profits. The truth, confirmed with depressing regularity throughout human history, is that, left to ourselves, we find it impossible to escape the hold of evil on our lives, both in a personal and a social way. One way is to give in to it and jam the yearning for ideal love and goodness with a busy noise of activity and distraction. Another way is to erect a fortified wall of cynicism and bitter resignation, inside which the natural yearning for reconciliation with a pure and loving goodness shrivels and dies.

But there is still another way. The God of love for whom we instinctively long, has come in person to let us escape from all the evil in and around us. We cannot buy this freedom; it is freely given through the abundance of his love.

JOHN 1:29-34

John knew that he was to prepare the people for the coming of the Messiah, even though he did not know who it was going to be. John had to trust God until God chose to reveal his next task: witnessing that Jesus was the Chosen One. Accordingly, he was given the necessary insight and understanding to enable him to witness with conviction.

We will often find ourselves being led by the Spirit in a similar way. We may be given some task to do and wish we knew where it is leading or how it can be of any use. If we simply trust God he will lead us step by step, allowing us to see just enough at a time to make our work possible. It may not be good for us to know too much at first; humans are impatient creatures, and may destroy God's plans by trying to complete them too hastily. We need to trust God more.

2nd Sunday after the Epiphany

Calling of the first disciples. Just as the prophets through the ages and the apostles were called by name by God to work with him for the good of the world, so we are chosen and called to work in partnership with God for the growth of his kingdom.

YEAR 1

JEREMIAH 1:4-10

Jeremiah does not feel up to God's calling: he is aware of his own inadequacies and the demanding nature of the job he has been given, and cannot believe he will have what it takes to make a good job of it. God reassures him (and us, too,) that he has set him apart for this even before his birth, and will himself provide the means to do well. With the symbolic gesture of touching Jeremiah's mouth, God consecrates his speech to be used as a channel of God's words.

ACTS 26:9-20

Paul seemed to be another unlikely candidate for helping the spread of the kingdom. He began by doing his pretty efficient best to stamp out the whole community of Jesus-followers before they could contaminate the world with their blasphemous teaching.

Once again, God calls. A witness coming from someone as hard to persuade as Paul is going to be a very powerful witness indeed, so God will actually be using Paul's energetic and misguided persecution for good. All he needs to bring resurrection out of death, is Paul's response. Very probably Stephen's example had prepared the ground; also Paul was a committed, prayerful Jew; the blinding realisation that Jesus really was God's Son flung him into a lifetime of spreading the Good News far and wide.

MARK 1:14-20

Jesus' call concerns repentance. This is always the necessary first step; nothing can happen, no growth can start at all, until we confess that we are to blame and our sinful way of going on is our own fault. The buck stops here.

If you recoil from the unpleasantness of full repentence you are not alone; neither are you misguided: taking the blame and renouncing excuses is a humiliating and painful experience. It hurts. But, as any dentist will confirm, no filling will be effective, not even a gold one, if the cavity is not first drilled clear of all decay.

After the bad news comes the Good News! A new life, confident, independent of circumstances, a fresh delight and enthusiasm, an outlook of hope and challenge. The fishermen left their old life and followed Jesus' call. Dare we do the same?

YEAR 2

I SAMUEL 3:1-10

Even before he was born, Samuel had been consecrated to the Lord; and now, while he is still a child, God calls him to prophesy. It would seem that few other people were receptive enough to hear the word of God, for it was 'rare' at that time. The priesthood had degenerated in greed and self-indulgence, with Eli's own two sons the worst offenders, and Eli had already been warned of God's retribution. He had spoken to his spoilt sons but had done nothing to put things right.

Samuel does not recognise God's voice straight away, and Eli, well-meaning but weak, recognises that God is speaking to this child and teaches him how to respond. So begins a lifetime of close communion with God; Samuel treasured the word of his Lord and always acted upon it, however unpleasant or unexpected it proved to be.

Communal worship is essential and of great value, but it is also vital to keep times of silence to commune with God, listen to his presence and respond to his calling.

GALATIANS 1:11-END

Paul gives us another example of someone who did not at first recognise God's voice. He thought he did. He was thoroughly committed to what he believed was God's will. But, still, he was persecuting the God he worshipped until his dramatic flash of understanding on the road to Damascus.

Having realised the truth of Jesus' claim to be the Son of the living God, Paul's entire life is handed over to the work of spreading the Good News that had taken him so long to grasp.

JOHN 1:35-END

Some time before being called to commit their whole lives to following Jesus, the disciples are directed to him by John the Baptist, who points him out as being the promised Lamb of God. They trail along behind him, rather than approaching him directly, until eventually he turns and asks them what they want. And isn't that so human? When we have the chance to meet someone we have longed to talk to and learn from, we become quite tongue-tied when we actually see them!

But Jesus is compassionate, welcoming, understanding and straightforward. Whenever he finds us hovering nearby, he will invite us to spend time with him and get to know him better. Then we can go and tell our family and friends news that will transform their lives, too.

3rd Sunday after the Epiphany

The way God's glory is shown through signs and miracles. Throughout the Old Testament God proves his love for his people by the care and protection he lavishes on them, and as Jesus heals, feeds and encourages his way through the Gospel, we become aware of his glory – the glory of God himself.

YEAR 1

EXODUS 33:12-END

One of the things that marked out the God of Moses as different from the nature gods of polytheism, was his real presence shown in actions and events of history (such as the escape from Egypt, or manna in the desert). In fact, it was this that made the Chosen People set apart – not because they were any better than any other nation (they very obviously weren't!) but that other nations could see that their God accompanied them personally.

This conversation between Moses and his Lord reveals their closeness and companionship, which is given special confirmation in the way God allows Moses a glimpse of his full glory, while he is shielded from harm by God's own hand. Our God may be the Lord of all power and all creative energy, but he is also the God of tenderness and warm affection.

I JOHN 1:1-7

John knows this from personal experience; he has actually witnessed the glory of God as revealed in the ministry of Jesus. He has seen something of God's compassion, love and personal concern for others in the kind of work Jesus did, the signs and miracles he gave and the unflinching love he showed. Such goodness is described as light, and those of us who claim to follow Jesus are bound to live in such light. If we only pay lip-service to the light then we live a lie. But within the light, in companionship with Jesus, we are given the resources to live in caring love with one another.

JOHN 2:1-11
In a sense, the miracle at Cana was a speeding up of the natural creative process. Water, in the form of rain, does indeed turn to wine through the slow growing, the sunshine, the fermenting and the maturing. Here Jesus is showing himself as Lord of time, in harmony with all growth and maturing, both in the natural and in the spiritual. He, then, has the power to mature us from water into wine.

YEAR 2

DEUTERONOMY 8:1-6
Moses reminds the people of the stages of their journey that have brought them to the present, rather as we might get out the old photograps on family occasions and watch the family's growth and change through the years. The relationship of God to his people is very much a family one – he is a kind, firm, wise and loving parent who has been guiding his children's development and cares about their future.

This personal involvement of a loving God is strikingly different from the pagan religions, and marks a new era in the spiritual development of humankind. The God of power and glory, from whom springs all creation, reveals himself in a loving relationship with the beings he has made.

PHILIPPIANS 4:10-20
If we let ourselves trust and depend on God's parental care, our happiness will become far less dependent on the colour of our bank balance or on material comforts and possessions. Like Paul, we shall be able to enjoy both richness and poverty, and be just as happy whether we have little or plenty.

God's glory will make itself known in his practical care of us in all circumstances.

Our materialistic society makes it difficult to latch on to Paul's outlook; we are pressurised by the media and social expectations, to be concerned about achieving better material comforts for ourselves and others, and to see health and wealth as necessary for happiness.

To train ourselves to delight in whatever God provides, it sometimes helps to make ourselves say, 'thank you, Lord' every time we miss a bus, spill our best whisky, cannot afford a new coat or use our holiday savings on repairing the car. Thankfulness is a habit, and when we remember to rejoice in the not-having as much as the having, we shall be much richer and, incidentally, happier.

JOHN 6:1-14

Perhaps Philip needed to learn to rely less on buying answers to problems and more on God's freely given grace. A rapid calculation makes it obvious that in this case, anyway, money is not going to work.

The small boy's quick and willing response, with a prompt offer of his own lunch, shows the lovely quality of children that Jesus warmed to and longed to find in adults. 'Use mine!' is so often the reaction even from young children, and as a parent it is touching to find a favourite teddy shoved eagerly in alongside Dad when he has 'flu; or their special comforter shared with Grandma after an operation.

Andrew is obviously touched by the boy's gift, but has natural adult misgivings about the actual use of it! But for Jesus, the willing offering, the spontaneous desire to sacrifice, is what enables him to feed the vast company of people with God's liberality. As soon as we show we are ready to put ourselves out, God can use us, often with far, far more effect than our meagre offering on its own could have achieved.

4th Sunday after the Epiphany

God shows his glory in our lives by renewing us from the inside and transforming us completely. As we increase our availability to the life-giving power of God, we shall become more and more like him, and reflect his glory more and more brightly.

YEAR 1

I KINGS 8:22-30

The splendid new temple has at last been completed in all its magnificence. The whole population has come to stand before God as it is dedicated. There is an excitement and hope pulsing through Solomon's prayer as he offers the house he has made. Solomon is acutely aware that any building, however beautiful, is insufficient a house for a God who planned and fashioned the vast and intricate universe.

Yet, though he is humbled by this, he is not overcome with despair or futility because he knows God's habit of using what we offer to dramatic effect. What is important, and must never be neglected, is the act of offering. Whatever we build in our lives – marriages, businesses, careers, relationships – all can be in-dwelt by the living God with remarkable effect, providing we dedicate them from the outset to the God who made all our efforts possible in the first place.

I CORINTHIANS 3:10-17

Foundations are all-important, and in our lives the only foundation possible for an effective and fruitful life is Jesus, the Christ. If we suddenly come to realise with dismay that we have been building with hay and straw, it will be necessary to dismantle down to the foundations before we can begin building again with stronger and better materials, which incidentally, God will always provide.

Sometimes we are so keen to do things our way that we scratch about for bits of straw so busily that we don't notice the fine stone God is offering for our use. Whenever we feel dispirited or overworked, it is worth stopping for a look at Jesus; it may be that we have not been using the best materials.

JOHN 2:13-22

Corruption never happens all at once. Gradually and insidiously the dealing in money-changing had encroached on the holiness of the temple – a sign of greed and selfishness creeping in, taking over the spiritual purity of God's people.

When we read this passage straight after Solomon's dedication prayer of the original temple, so many years before, the sordid difference between high ideals and squabbling, corrupt practice, we can understand Jesus' zeal in driving out all the dealers and moneychangers from God's house. It is an anger fired by love for people who are bent on their own spiritual destruction; a sign of how drastic and thorough repentance needs to be, both in an individual and in a nation. As some of the good kings of Israel had atoned for religious corruption by smashing all idols and destroying cult worship, so Jesus publicly cleanses the temple before atoning for all sin by his sacrifice on the cross. Only through systematic crucifying of sin and selfishness can resurrection life in us flourish.

YEAR 2

JEREMIAH 7:1-11

Jeremiah never minced his words! He was one of those people who refuse to be lulled into accepting lax standards just because they have become the usual practice, and here he derides the hypocrisy of those who pay lip service to God's law when at the temple, but whose corrupt lives are a blatant denial of it.

The hypocrisy of living a lie is a base insult to the purity and integrity of God, and renders our worship void and ludicrous. If our worship seems dead on its feet, no novelties or flashy gimmicks will revive it; but it will burst into life spontaneously and become flooded with meaning and vitality whenever there is a thorough and rigorous repentance and a genuine seeking after God.

HEBREWS 12:18-END

The writer compares our revelation of God with God's revelation to Moses and the people of Israel. The experience of the Old Testament was awesome and terrifying; for us, in the light of Christ, the kingdom of heaven itself is open to us, if only we will take it, and that is something which should inspire us to utmost reverence and awe.

It is only when we truly humble ourselves before God in spirit that true worship can begin, and our lives can be gradually transformed and made new through God's power.

JOHN 4:19-26

The new life, with all its vitality, freedom and peace, is available to everyone of every nationality, not just the chosen race to whom and through whom it was first brought. The Samaritan woman is drawn to question Jesus about the issues which worry her and make her angry, until gradually she is led to see that all these wranglings are submerged in the greater significance of God's eventual purpose for his creation. Pure worship begins in the heart, and its effect on lives is shown personally in the life of Jesus of Nazareth.

5th Sunday after the Epiphany

The wisdom of God is revealed to us clearly in Jesus. Through all the problems and decision-making of our lives we have God's assurance that he will lead us to make good choices and act wisely and well, provided we remain rooted in the loving wisdom of our Lord.

YEARS 1 AND 2

PROVERBS 2:1-9

In these words of advice it is the seeking which is important and will gradually lead to a depth of understanding and knowledge of God. We are reminded of the emphasis Jesus also placed on committed, diligent seeking, along with his promise that if we do seek we shall certainly find.

As Christians, all our life-journey is a seeking after the mind of God, and we are in great danger of complacency if ever we start to think we have arrived. For God encompasses so much that we can never tie him down to a limited space, the shape of our imaginations or hopes. Rather, our search will draw us gradually deeper into fellowship with God, and each new insight will open up new terrain to discover within the loving God who created us.

or

ECCLESIASTICUS 42:15-END

This beautiful passage opens our eyes to see God's remarkable creation with the freshness of newly-acquired vision. So often we take it all for granted because we are used to it, and fail to see in the material world all the signs and symbols of God's abundant glory. There are dark, deep and secret places spiritually as well as materially; infinite space reflects the infinite time of eternity; the life-giving brightness of the sun expresses the life-creating power and love of God. We can train our eyes to see only the unsatisfactory, the wrong or the novel; or we can train them to recognise also all the wonder, wisdom and glory of God.

I CORINTHIANS 3:18-END

Being full of Christ's love, we are like holy temples, filled with the presence of God. When we remember this it can comfort us during danger and strengthen us when we are tempted to abuse our bodies.

For we do not belong to ourselves any more, but to Christ, and when that still point is fixed, all other loyalties and commitments will fall into place. No personality or theory is as important as our relationship with Christ.

MATTHEW 12:38-42

There is a world of difference between seeking God and looking rather ghoulishly for signs. Signs are exciting, dramatic and 'easy' because they require nothing except a few Ooh's and Ah's. Jesus knew right at the start of his ministry that such showmanship would draw the crowds – hence his temptation to use the technique when Satan suggested he should throw himself off the temple pinnacle and be unharmed.

But Jesus rejected the idea. He prefers to coax and encourage us, step by step, teaching us faith by the very act of our searching, increasing our insight and perception through our desire to see more clearly.

6th Sunday after the Epiphany

God's character is revealed through parables to all who seek to know him more clearly. Jesus often used the form of parables – stories with hidden meanings – as an aid to teaching people about God and the kingdom of heaven.

YEARS 1 AND 2

2 SAMUEL 12:1-10

Whenever we embark on a course that is wrong, we are very likely to justify our actions to ourselves so as to quieten the nagging voice of conscience. It is quite possible to do this so effectively that we silence our conscience, with disastrous hardening of heart as a result.

Thankfully, before David has accomplished this, Nathan approaches him through the power of a parable, which forces him to see the truth of his sin objectively. We all tend to be extra indignant about sins which are actually part of our own behaviour, and David is outraged by the behaviour of the rich man in Nathan's story.

Now, when Nathan confronts him with the full horror of his own behaviour, David is challenged. He can either turn away from the truth and run from God into the dark prison of self, or he can repent, and run weeping towards the God of purity and love.

ROMANS 1:18-25

God's world shows order and discipline from the spiralling galaxies down to the structures of DNA; Paul argues that there is plenty of evidence to point us in God's direction, even if we do not recognise him by name. Our consciences can direct us to respecting one another, caring unselfishly for one another and using the world's riches wisely.

If we persist in self-indulgence, and close our eyes to the truth, we can expect a spread of violence and evil, a sense of futility pervading society; darkness and degradation in a restless world.

MATTHEW 13:24-30

While in this life we may well find that weeds and thorns seem to be flourishing better than the wheat. Incredible sums of money change hands for things which are of little lasting value; dubious entertainers and money jugglers are highly paid and esteemed by many, while less glamorous yet infinitely valuable and caring work is poorly paid and unacclaimed.

If we are tempted to be hurt by the injustice of how, often, evil appears to receive all the rewards, we can re-read this parable which acknowledges that good and evil must grow alongside each other until the end of time, when only what is good will survive.

9th Sunday before Easter

Christ the teacher. Not only with his words, but in his life Jesus shows us how to live fulfilled and fruitful lives, realising our potential and playing our part in bringing the world to wholeness.

YEAR 1

ISAIAH 30:18-21

Isaiah had been given a vision of a world in which God's kingdom was established and so he is able to speak to the people with hope and encouragement. His words would be fulfilled more practically than even he himself imagined.

For when Jesus taught his followers in Galilee so many generations later, he took Isaiah's words and applied them to himself; he was the voice which says to us 'I am the Way, follow me'. His offer means that everyone can have a personal itinerary through life – an individually structured route with a personal guide and companion.

I CORINTHIANS 4:8-13

The Corinthian Christians had become complacent. Their comfortable lifestyle had not increased their spiritual perception, and their values had therefore become somewhat distorted. We can imagine them looking down on the vagrant, unglamorous lives of the missionaries like Paul who have often been prepared to look like fools for the sake of spreading the teaching of Christ.

Paul reminds them that Christ's idea of wealth is rather different. Christians are not promised any kind of worldly security; it is expected that they will often be abused, passed over and insulted. But part of their teaching will be the way they put up with hardship cheerfully, accept criticism patiently, and repay insults with courtesy.

MATTHEW 5:1-12

When we grasp the meaning of the first beatitude, the others follow on from it. If we put God first and regard ourselves not as possessors but stewards of worldly goods, we shall be poor (or unpossessive) in spirit. That will make us less aggressive, defensive and ambitious, so we become more gentle in our dealings with others.

Those who are gentle are more sympathetic, and that makes us vulnerable, affected by the pain around us, so we shall find ourselves mourning, due to more loving involvement. Seeing the causes of suffering will make us long to put right the areas of injustice and cruelty which harm and damage, so that we shall hunger and thirst after righteousness.

Yet, loving oppressors as well as the oppressed, we shall want to act with God's mercy, rather than fighting for good with the weapons of evil. Such involvement will make us increasingly aware of the contrast between God's purity and the chaotic corruption of misdirected humanity, which is bound, in turn, to inspire us to work towards peace, reconciliation and love.

Once we are set on that route, as history bloodily endorses, we are bound for the cross; and having stuck our necks out, we are targets for persecution.

Yet the journey has been one towards greater and greater closeness to the Spirit of God; towards the peace of knowing we are doing his will; towards finding our true selves and serving him. And that is certain happiness.

YEAR 2

PROVERBS 3:1-8

This is the kind of sound advice we may feel like giving our children as they leave home for the first time! With God at the centre of life we shall be able to pick our way through all the traumas and disasters, temptations and failures – not avoiding them, necessarily, but growing through them in compassion and wisdom rather than being beaten down by them.

I CORINTHIANS 2:1-10

The Greeks were used to philosophical arguments. They prided themselves on their civilised discussions and persuasion by logic and, up to a point, the existence of God can be argued in this way.

But when the uncompromising love of God floods into our life in the person of Jesus, culminating in the crucifixion and resurrection, there comes a point at which even philosophy is swept away in the wash.

Paul shows the Corinthians how he is quite content being a nervous and unremarkable preacher because it highlights the evidence of God himself – the outpouring of his Spirit of love. With less chance of his hearers giving Paul glory they are more likely to direct their praise to God.

LUKE 8:4B-15

Even when God actually walked the earth as a man, many did not notice the obvious, because their inner eyes and ears were shut fast by complacency and lack of desire to change in any way.

None of this alters the quality of the seed itself, which, if it falls on good, rich soil, can produce an excellent crop. But the parable emphasises other factors involved – our own response, perseverance, capacity to trust and our willingness to be committed wholeheartedly.

It is a good idea to use this parable sometimes during self-examination, as, of course, there is always the possibility of even good soil becoming stony or choked with weeds!

8th Sunday before Easter

Jesus as the healer. The prophets had foretold the time when God's healing love would renew and restore, and whenever holy men and women became channels of God's power, acts of healing had occurred which directed the people's praise towards the God of creation and renewal. Now, in Jesus, God walks among his people, restoring them to wholeness.

YEAR 1

ZEPHANIAH 3:14-END

This reading proclaims, with exultant hope and joy, that when the Lord our God is right here in the midst of us, all things are well and there is no evil we need fear. Think of Paul and Silas, beaten with rods and imprisoned with their feet in the stocks; they spent the night praying and singing, entertaining the other prisoners! When we ask God to give us the assurance of his presence he often responds by filling us with a quite unexpected joy, not at all in keeping with the pain we are suffering. For his healing reaches the parts other healing cannot reach: God's healing is wholeness.

JAMES 5:13-16A

James always gives practical help and advice, and when people are feeling weak and vulnerable through their illness, this is just what they need. The Christian community has a responsibility to undertake the visiting of the sick, both at home and in hospital, and not just during the time of a health crisis. In many illnesses there is a long stage of convalescence during which the bustle and activity of emergency has gone, and this can be a lonely and demoralising time. We need to meet the need for companionship and encouragement right through to full recovery.

MARK 2: 1-12

Jesus always heals in the way that brings most lasting good. As in a symphony, many parts are merged in harmony. So often God's way of answering prayer touches far more lives with blessing than the solution we had envisaged.

Here the remarkable faith of the paralytic's friends allows Jesus to touch the raw nerves of suspicion in the scribes, and gives them the opportunity to believe in him as God's chosen one for whom they have been waiting.

The friends do not murmur when Jesus forgives the man instead of enabling him to walk straight away, because they trust him, and their trust makes them patient and accepting. For the scribes, this met their suspicions head on. They knew that only God has power to forgive sins. What a wonderful opportunity Christ gave them, here, in immediately following his absolution with healing. What joy there might have been if this direct, startling proof had been sufficient for them! We need to pray that our eyes will be able to discern the power of God in action. Closed minds face the bleak prospect of failing to recognise the only one who can save them.

YEAR 2

2 KINGS 5:1-14

If it hadn't been for the little servant girl from Israel, Naaman would never have set off hopefully to find Elisha. When God heals, he uses many people and many circumstances along the way, and we never know when we are going to be in a position to help. If we get into the habit of praying wherever we happen to be, God will be able to use us for his healing work in ways we may never even be aware of. Not just physical healing; a letter of appreciation or encouragement may arrive just at a low point in someone's life.

Elisha's prayerfulness kept him in close touch both with God's will, and Naaman's need.

2 CORINTHIANS 12:1-10

Often after a deep spiritual experience, which sets us off full of enthusiasm to spread our faith more, we may find ourselves meeting obstacles!

When you think about it, that is not really surprising, as the last thing Satan wants is for us to bring more people to Christ's saving love. Paul's list of insults and sufferings gives us some idea of what to expect, and is not exactly inviting.

However, the strangest paradox becomes evident as soon as we set ourselves to do his will. The more difficult life is, the easier it seems to be to witness to others in an effective way that really draws them to our Lord. Hanging on to his hand for dear life, we experience such overwhelming support and such miracles of perfect timing, answered prayers and peace of mind, that we can witness to actual knowledge of a God who is alive and well, interested in us enough to want to help and remake us. There is only one conclusion we can draw: he must really love us! After that, the difficulties matter less; if they keep us relying on the Lord we love and who loves us, then we are happy to have things that way.

MARK 7:24-END

Spittle was commonly used in the medicine of Jesus' time, so it is interesting that his healing incorporated this. When we pray for healing, our prayer may well be answered via a visit to the doctor or the hospital, for God delights in using us and our gifts in the work of healing. Every time researchers discover new ways to combat pain and disease, that is a victory for the God of Wholeness who enlightens and heals.

If we really want to see Jesus in action, we have only to visit a patient who has been 'prayed through' a major operation; their radiance shows plainly that wholeness is more than clinical health; that Jesus personally transforms the spiritual, emotional and physical structure of the people he is asked to heal.

7th Sunday before Easter

Jesus Christ as the friend of sinners. The bad news about being human is that we seem to find it so easy to hurt one another and indulge in our selfishness; with even the best of intentions, we fail and sin. The good news is that in Jesus, God meets us where we are, loves us, warts and all, and brings about reconciliation, forgiveness and peace.

YEAR 1

HOSEA 14:1-7

The northern kingdom was fast approaching the threat of collapse after generations of unfaithfulness, self-indulgence and decadence. As the prophet Amos had pointed out, they deserved all they were going to get, for they had rejected God utterly, and God would be quite justified in abandoning them to their fate. But Hosea, personally wounded by his own beloved but unfaithful wife, was able to balance the justice of God's character with his tender mercy and forgiving love. He is the loving and faithful husband of his people, and though deeply hurt and grieved by them, he is always willing to start afresh with them and welcome them back.

PHILEMON 1-16

Jesus' spirit of forgiveness is seen working here in a way we may recognise from our own experience. Just as paintwork on the house requires a lot of careful preparation before the final coating of gloss can gleam, so forgiveness of deep hurts will take patience, hard work and encouragement before full reconciliation is achieved. We need not be ashamed to admit that it is taking us time to forgive; if we are genuinely working on it in Jesus' strength the time will come when we will know there is complete healing, and this honest approach is far better than pretending our wound is healed when really it festers as bitterness deep inside us.

Like Paul, we can often help ease the way between hurt and reconciliation by looking at the good in people so regularly that it becomes a habit; by refusing to join in critical gossip; and by being positive and encouraging instead of destructive.

MARK 2:13-17

It is such a relief to find that with Jesus, at least, we are totally accepted for what we are, and although he is totally good and sinless, he will happily make himself at home with us, even though he knows our worst as well as our best points.

There is a touch of sarcasm in Jesus' reply to the offended Pharisees and teachers of the law. For by thinking themselves so superior, they were cutting themselves off from the possibility of healing. Even if you are seriously ill, you will never get treatment if you insist you are perfectly well and don't need the doctor.

The truth, of course, is that we all need the healing reconciliation with God that Jesus has the power to give.

YEAR 2

NUMBERS 15:32-36

Life in the wilderness was dangerous and hard, and in order to survive at all, self-discipline was essential. The ten commandments gave the people a moral structure which reflected their trust in and dependence on God, and it was vital that God's law was taken seriously and kept faithfully.

So it is in these circumstances that the man is punished so severely for breaking God's law of keeping the Sabbath day set apart, or holy, to God. In context, then, it is a just punishment. Jesus, however, was to show that God's justice is always mingled with compassion.

COLOSSIANS 1:18-23

In Christ we are brought into a new understanding of God's cosmic significance. For Christ's actions reveal God's plan to unify, reconcile and overcome all powers of evil and destruction, so that we may no longer be held in their grip.

In Christ we are liberated from any power of the occult, from temporal tyranny and cruelty and even from what grips us most tightly: our own sin.

So we can afford to be filled with joy, laughter, and relaxed peacefulness, because we have just been let out of prison where we were in the condemned cell awaiting death! And the one to thank for it is Jesus Christ, who accomplished it by dying in our place, even though he was innocent. That shows quite a staggering capacity for love.

JOHN 8:2-11

We are now shown an illustration of God's forgiveness in the episode of the woman taken in adultery. She was dragged by the indignant crowd before this new teacher, and she stood in front of him as a convicted person, condemned already to death by stoning according to the Law. Jesus does not excuse her, nor does he pretend she has done nothing wrong. He quietly and shrewdly points out to the crowd that all stand condemned by the law, for all have sinned. (Notice how it is the oldest member who is the first to realise this!)

When everyone has gone, Jesus 'redeems' the woman from her conviction and wipes out the sin of her past. Now she is free and told not to sin again in the future: before her is a completely new life.

To have her death sentence removed must have been wonderful enough; but to have her guilt and sin removed at the same time must have been utterly overwhelming.

Ash Wednesday

Reconciliation with God. This will involve first admitting our need of God's mercy and forgiveness and then examining our lives in his light to see what needs to be done. God does not simply patch up the bits of us that look bad – he completely renews and restores, giving us the joy and peace of forgiveness.

YEARS 1 AND 2

ISAIAH 58:1-8 OR JOEL 2:12-17 OR AMOS 5:6-15

In all these readings, sincerity of the heart is crucial. Outward hysterical drama of tearing clothes or showy breast-beating is not necessary. Other people may be impressed by it, but God is never fooled. He sees clearly the hidden, secret thoughts in our hearts; and it is the complete altering of our values, so that God becomes central, that makes his forgiveness effective.

It is so easy, while life flows smoothly along, to become complacent, almost without realising it. Although we may deplore the jolts and tragedies that make open sores in our well-ordered lives, they may sometimes do us a great service.

Whenever our timetable is disrupted, it challenges us about whose order really underpins our life; every time material possessions are lost or stolen we are challenged as to where our real treasure is on which our hearts are fixed.

These challenges are very good for us, and provide marvellous opportunities for relinquishing another layer of independence from God and committing ourselves to him more deeply.

From time to time this needs to be a great communal act of repentance and recommitment. There may be potential within the whole parish which is not being realised; needs which are not being met; opportunities which are not being taken.

The way forward in all Christian communities is through thorough, heart-searching repentance. This alone can open the way to God's forgiveness, leading to stronger, more vigorous growth, and lots more fruit.

I CORINTHIANS 9:24-END OR JAMES 4:1-10

These readings deal with the practical business of putting things right. For repentance is not the end of the matter but the beginning. Just as we have to put considerable effort into becoming physically fit, so we need to be rigorous and organised about our spiritual fitness, which has, after all, got to last us not just for a lifetime but for ever!

And just as muscles protest when we start training them, so we shall find it painful at times being re-made as God's children. Don't despair, at such times, but rejoice, because the pain is proof of progress and is making you spiritually strong and healthy.

MATTHEW 6:16-21 OR LUKE 18:9-14

Jesus saw around him, among the religious community, some who did the right things for the wrong reasons. To him, looking with the discernment of God, it was quite obvious which ones were acting and what they were really after in their almsgiving, praying and fasting. They were being just subtle enough to take in those whose admiration they craved, and as a result, were highly respected.

Sometimes we use even more subtle ways of pocketing the glory which belongs to God. Perhaps we casually let slip our good deeds in conversation, or recount our news with a heavy editorial slant in favour of Number One. It is quite a useful exercise to attempt to do three good deeds in a day without anyone ever finding out!

Of course, it all stems from the heart; if we are primarily concerned with serving God and pleasing him, we need not become neurotic about what others see or do not see. Their reactions will cease to be so important, and if they do notice us shining, we can gladly and willingly direct the praise to God in whose strength we live.

1st Sunday in Lent

Temptation. Man and woman spoilt God's perfect creation by falling into temptation and disobeying their creator. We are all guilty of sin, but through Christ we are given the strength and grace to resist temptation just as he did.

YEAR 1

GENESIS 2:7-9; 3:1-7

Nakedness always suggests vulnerability; in our clothes we can, to some extent, choose the image we present to the world, but naked we are just ourselves, as at birth and death. This is why we usually need a relationship of trust before we are at ease being naked in company; yet where this happens, as in family groups, for instance, there is no doubt that the nakedness points to a special, trusting relationship there.

When Adam and Eve were suddenly embarrassed by their nakedness it showed that their special, trusting relationship with their creator had been damaged and spoilt. They knew they had been disobedient and they were ashamed; much as we find it hard to meet people's eyes directly if we know we have wronged them in some way.

HEBREWS 2:14-END

Jesus came so that we could once more stand naked before God, without trying to hide any part of our bodies or characters; so that, as children, we could have a secure relationship with him based on love and acceptance.

The only way this could be done was for the profound disobedience to be reversed. Someone had to go through all the temptations but still resist the urge to disobey God's will.

Someone did it. What happened to that person was the agony of betrayal, torture and crucifixion, resulting in death. But it was, in another way, life; for Jesus went right through to the farthest edge of human temptation and suffering and yet still remained absolutely obedient. He hung naked before his heavenly father at that moment of human death, and in so doing won back for us the long lost relationship with God that Adam and Eve had been created to enjoy.

MATTHEW 4:1-11

Some of the main temptations Jesus had to resist were, naturally, aimed at the weakest areas, and they all had just enough relationship with good sense to make them dangerous. After all, if someone approached us proposing a brutal act of murder we should not find that very hard to resist; but if we are persuaded that a dishonest act is going to harm no one and will benefit those we love, then the moral issues blur and it is much harder to see and resist temptation.

As with Adam and Eve, hunger is used, and the great advantage of immediate, dramatic results. 'You will be like gods,' Adam and Eve were persuaded. Jesus, knowing he had power, was urged to behave like a man-god, pandering to our craving for excitement, but ignoring our real needs.

In resisting these temptations Jesus was abandoning any possibility of a peaceful end to his life; instead he kept the door wide open for our salvation.

YEAR 2

GENESIS 4:1-10

Resentment can be a killer. Sometimes it results in murder, as in Cain's case. Always it rubs and festers deep inside us, damaging our capacity for love and destroying our peace. Any seething hatred we harbour for anyone, however much they may have hurt us, will probably damage us more than it does them, so it needs to be lanced and healed as quickly and thoroughly as possible.

There are times when we all feel scared by the capacity for evil we suddenly glimpse in ourselves; it can seem far bigger than we are and threaten to crush us. Thankfully, good already has the victory through Jesus, and we can cling on to that strength of his until Satan slinks away.

HEBREWS 4:12-END

Jesus can provide such strength because he has been through the very worst possible experience of overpowering evil and remained sinless. It is with the confidence of this knowledge that we are able to approach God and make use of his deep reserves of grace and unlimited mercy.

LUKE 4:1-13

Jesus was also fully human, so the temptations were excruciatingly real and just as hard to resist as the temptations which face us. And they were couched in such a way that falling into the trap could be rationalised and even appear justifiable.

First, Jesus was hungry and weak. He knew he was entrusted with great power, and he was in great need. Surely it would be sensible to use just a little of that power to alleviate physical suffering?

And then there was the desire to draw all men to God. Perhaps, after all, being a kind of Superman might be one way of attracting all those people who wouldn't be interested in things like humility, patience or repentance.

Then there was the urgency of his work; having only a lifetime, if that, to save God's people, perhaps a ministry of worldly power and influence might be quicker.

How, then, did he manage, as man, to resist such temptations? He was able to resist them because he was never, at any point, separated from the power of God.

The weakness of our humanity will often be threatened and tempted. But our access to God's almighty power means that in Christ we shall have the necessary strength to cope.

2nd Sunday in Lent

The conflict between right and wrong. We need discernment to recognise God's will on our journey through an often confusing and disturbing world. Following Jesus demands both trust and calm, level-headed assessment of anyone setting him or herself up as a prophet or spiritual leader. If we learn to look with the eyes of Christ, we shall not be led astray.

YEAR 1

GENESIS 6:11-END

Noah put faith in God's promises and survived with his family in spite of the devastating flood. No doubt he had had to put up with lots of jokes at his expense as the people continued to live corrupt and careless lives while he and his sons got busy with the wood and pitch. Such concern with obeying God's wishes would seem to many a waste of time and energy, while life went on as usual.

Through his prayer (which, incidentally, involved quite as much listening as talking) Noah was able to keep in touch with God's will even while living among the many distractions of a worldly society. His example can encourage us when our faith seems to make us outsiders.

I JOHN 4:1-6

Trustfulness is often emphasised as a Christian virtue, and indeed we do need the young child's straightforward trust which is so endearing. But it is important to remember that this trust is not a naivety which accepts unquestioningly and is blown this way and that by different advice, and is easy prey for the cunning or unscrupulous.

As responsible, rational beings, we are urged to use our God-given intelligence and common sense to examine any claims and teaching of religious leaders to distinguish between those speaking God's truth and those who are not. We are not to follow blindly, under pressure or on an emotional 'high'. God is not shallow; if the claims are true they will stand up to close scrutiny. Both the preacher's words and the fruit of his or her life should bear witness to the fact that Jesus the Christ, made flesh, came from God.

LUKE 19:41-END

Jesus is heartbroken by the sight of Jerusalem, set to be the city of light which would draw all nations to the knowledge of God's love; instead the people have failed to recognise their king and redeemer, and their blindness is launching them headfirst towards destruction.

Surely he weeps still over all the chances and opportunities we carelessly discard; all the evidence of his glory we are too busy to notice; and all the meaningless trivialities that make the highest claims on our time, talents and money.

YEAR 2

GENESIS 7:17-END

Purposely the passage chosen for today finishes before the flood recedes, with all the hope and promise of the rainbow glowing in the sky. It is good to know that all will be well, but at the moment we are concerned with how we all feel at crisis points in our lives. Noah and his family have watched the terrible anguish of many terrified people drowning. Their compassion and sorrow are mixed with relief and joy at being alive through God's help. The familiar world is utterly devastated and the future completely unknown. So here they drift, buoyed up but without direction, and all they are to do is wait for the water to subside. Such patient waiting can be used as a prayer in itself; God's love will buoy us up even when we are adrift because of pain, grief or some shattering of our lives.

I JOHN 3:1-10

A person's actions display what he or she is really like; they really do speak louder than words. This is why you find out who your real friends are when times are hard: they will be the ones who stick around and help instead of fading conveniently into the distance.

As children of God, loving, caring behaviour is expected of us because that is the way Jesus behaved. The more time we spend with him, the more like him we will become. (You've seen it happen with dogs and their owners!) It is very exciting to think that the ordinary, familiar person you see in the mirror each morning is gradually being transformed into the likeness of the most loving, generous, responsive person ever.

MATTHEW 12:22-32

As if time is squeezed, we can watch this transforming process from physical illness to health, at the hands of Jesus. Amazement and wonder lead many to dare to speculate as to whether this healer can possibly be the Messiah. His ability to bring good out of evil is acting as a signpost. It would be impossible for an evil force to overthrow itself, so the effective act is proof of the presence of goodness and love.

3rd Sunday in Lent

The good news about suffering. In Christ, suffering can become a positive experience; a route to full life and deeper understanding. In fact, Jesus goes so far as to say it is a necessary part of our life in him. He will be there with us all through the very blackest, bleakest times.

YEAR 1

GENESIS 22:1-13

It must have seemed utterly incomprehensible to Abraham that God should ask him to sacrifice the very son through whom the promise of a chosen nation was to be fulfilled. If Isaac were killed, how could God's word possibly come true?

Perhaps Abraham was on the edge of trusting more in the means of achieving results than in the source of the power. Such a drastic threat to the 'means' threw Abraham's faith squarely onto the author of the promise. Since he was prepared to sacrifice even his beloved son, Abraham proved that even his most cherished hopes were second to his desire to serve God faithfully.

It was not any blood-sacrifice that God required; he needed the sacrifice of faith in other things, however closely those things may be tied up with his will. And it is all too easy to start trusting in the means instead of the source. If anything seems to be steering our attention away from God, we may find we are asked to abandon it, even though it is intrinsically good. Perhaps, once we have refocused our priorities, it will be given back abundantly; but by that time we will have sacrificed our faith in it, so our trust in God will have grown.

COLOSSIANS 1:24-END

Paul proclaims the fact that Christ is actually among us now; he is our guest and we are privileged to see his glory in a more personal, open way than any of the Old Testament prophets could.

His presence brings great joy and strength, but it also challenges us to join Christ in his redeeming work. This will certainly create problems, hardships and suffering in our lives, but since Christ, in person, has commissioned us, we can take up the work gladly, knowing he will support and uphold us always.

LUKE 9:18-27

Not surprisingly, when the people were faced with the promised Christ in person, they were full of suggestions about his identity which would not demand too shattering a change to their lives and beliefs. When Peter acknowledged Christ as God's chosen one, he was taking a tremendous risk. After all, at this stage there had been no resurrection, and Jesus looked and functioned in a perfectly normal way. To acknowledge Jesus as 'the Christ of God' meant unavoidable and radical change in Peter. The years of waiting had a certain safety about them, but if the Messiah was actually there standing next to him, the waiting was over and humanity had entered a new phase in the relationship with God.

Straight away, Jesus speaks of the inevitable action of suffering and death. There is no possible way to save the world other than the Creator himself submitting to his creation in an entire self-offering of love.

YEAR 2

GENESIS 12:1-9

Abram's obedience is so simply told that it sounds quite easy. In fact, it must have been a great upheaval and a move which was no doubt ridiculed as senseless by many; why did he want to uproot everything and wander off, leaving all his security behind, for goodness' sake?

Obviously Abram was not like a reed in the wind, easily persuaded by anybody. So he must have recognised that this calling, though unusual and unexpected, was nonetheless full of authority. He sensed the greatness of God, and bowed before it, committing his future security and welfare to God's protection.

If we say that we acknowledge God's greatness, then we must show it to be true in the way we willingly submit to changes, new directions, dangerous or unpleasant undertakings, without grumbling about what we have had to give up.

Whenever we are called forward we shall have to leave something behind. But God will be going with us, so we shall end up not poorer, but richer.

1 PETER 2:19-END

People often talk loosely of the cross they have to bear, when they mean one of the many hardships which are simply part of being human. But that cannot be what Jesus meant by taking up our crosses and following him. For him and us it signified a willingness to face and undergo persecution and death if necessary even when we are not guilty of what our accusers claim. And that, as Peter says, is where the merit lies, as far as God is concerned.

We are able to take as our example and prototype Christ, the suffering servant, who did not condemn or retaliate or even defend himself; instead he trusted in an eternal defence against which death is a powerless weapon. Drawing together the two aspects of purification symbolised by the scapegoat and sacrificed goat of the Jewish people, Jesus is both sent off into the wilderness, laden with our sin, and also offered as a pure victim as he dies a sinless death. He is therefore the complete atonement for reconciling us to God, for he is both human and divine.

MATTHEW 16:13-END

It is quite encouraging, in a way, to find that Peter, who was so obviously close to God and had such faith, also had times of blindness, when his thinking was not aligned with God's mind. Saints are not born perfect, but are very ordinary people like us.

Why was Jesus so quick to stamp on what Peter said? He was, after all, showing love and concern for Jesus, and it seems a natural reaction if a loved friend talks of walking openly into certain death. So why was Peter wrong? He was thinking with the mind of man; the concern for his loved friend and master was not wrong in itself but it did not go nearly far enough. It became trapped at the immediate instead of going further to see sacrifice as necessary for the much wider context of all humanity. And it therefore pulled the human Christ towards immediate, smaller gains and away from the very costly, divine plan for mankind's salvation.

There is, in other words, an element of grit and rigour in thinking God's way which may lead to a harder, longer and more expensive course of action than seems necessary to those around us. But if we find God asking such costly action of us, it is only because the long-term effects, perhaps on us or perhaps on society, will be immeasurably greater.

4th Sunday in Lent

God's glory, shown in Jesus at the transfiguration. The disciples were given glimpses of Jesus' divinity which strengthened their faith and upheld them. Through their account, we also become witnesses: Jesus is indeed the Son of God.

YEAR 1

EXODUS 34:29-END

The transfiguration of Christ is prefigured in the way Moses' face glows brightly after talking with the Lord. Their relationship is so close and deep that Moses 'catches' God's glory, and it shows.

Although Moses had remarkable gifts, he also had faults, and there is no attempt to make out that he was perfect. So it was not any freak, inimitable goodness that enabled Moses to draw so close to his God. It was only his longing to serve and love God with his whole being – heart, soul and body – that gradually drew him closer to the mind and heart of God.

2 CORINTHIANS 3:4-END

Handwriting gives away aspects of our character; so do the clothes we feel comfortable in. But, more than anything, our character is shown in the way we behave – the way we act and react in the different circumstances of our daily lives. Perhaps we have sometimes seen a good Christian person we would like to emulate, and tried to graft their way of behaving, like a package deal, on to ourselves. It never works, of course! There is no short cut to being a shining, effective Christian.

But the more we allow his Spirit to write on our hearts, the more effective witnesses we shall be. It will be a testimonial which is unique, since God loves us personally, and the in-dwelling of his Spirit simply makes us more fully ourselves. A lively Christian community, then, will be a very colourful collection of people, with a whole range of variety.

LUKE 9:28-36

This great transfiguring power of God was seen by the disciples as Jesus prayed on the mountain. It was beyond their understanding; but it must have remained, simmering in their minds, all through the humiliating crucifixion, till it burst out at the resurrection in an excited realisation that God had fulfilled his side of the promise, and anyone who was prepared to accept that promise could now be assured of an eventual transfiguration such as they had once witnessed. God, in Jesus, had proved it would happen.

Year 2
EXODUS 3:1-6

Fire is frequently used as a sign, or symbol of God's presence, and here Moses is given a powerful sense of God's presence which attracts him and yet fills him with fear. God identifies himself as being personal. He has been involved and concerned with every stage of his people's history. Spiritual experiences of his presence, not only for Moses but also for us, lead on to action which will draw the world closer to its creator.

2 PETER 1:16-19

We have Peter's eye-witness account of the transfiguration. The event has obviously had a tremendous impact on him, and given him assurance of faith which he passes on to his readers. At the time, Peter had wanted to 'fix' the experience, providing holy shrines for Jesus, Moses and Elijah. Of course, he couldn't hang on to it in that way, but this letter makes it clear that the transfiguration had in fact been indelibly fixed for ever by transfiguring Peter himself from the inside!

MATTHEW 17:1-13

Jesus was quite probably transfigured like this whenever he became rapt in prayer, but normally he sought out lonely places and prayed privately. On this occasion he allowed three of his closest followers to witness his godliness, and the sight stunned and strengthened them with its intense purity, and unblemished loveliness.

Sometimes, when we are deeply touched by a glorious sunset, or our children singing their best, for instance, we glimpse a reflection of God's glory. If we can train our senses to see it in all kinds of small, everyday occurrences we shall be richer, more thankful and happier people.

For our God is so great, so full of purity and perfection that we need not hold ourselves back in lavishing all our worship on him. We have within us an instinctive need and longing to lavish worth and adoration on something or someone.

Here, in Christ, we find the true object for all the love we long to give. We were made for it, that is why worshipping God brings such peace and joy.

5th Sunday in Lent

The victory of the cross. Nothing could look more like failure than the crucifixion, as the promising healer and teacher hung suffering at the mercy of mankind. Yet it was through this anguish and pain, offered in love without sin, that our salvation was secured for ever.

YEAR 1

EXODUS 6:2-13

The Israelites had become worn down and demoralised through cruelty and oppression. To them God seemed distant and irrelevant to their troubles. We, too, may well have experienced this, when circumstances are so difficult that we feel we need all our energies just to survive, and any message of hope seems a useless diversion. But God had not forgotten his people, any more than he ever forgets us. He has watched their suffering and shared in it, waiting only for the right time and receptive hearts in order to act. Now, through Moses and Aaron, the exodus from slavery can begin.

COLOSSIANS 2:8-15

God intervenes at his own expense to cancel the debt of sin. He does not lower his standards to accept man's dismal record of habitual sinning. After all, he knows man's potential and longs for him to know happiness and peace. So the only way he can cancel the debt is by paying it himself, in full. In the agony of the passion, we see this sacrifice in action, but this is only the historical focus of it: in terms of eternity, that debt is constantly being paid off; we see the suffering Christ in every starving, maltreated, exiled face.

Having paid the debt, Christ was raised and lives for ever; the first Easter Day was the historical focus, but in terms of eternity that resurrection victory continues too, in every barrier of hatred, broken by love.

JOHN 12:20-32

When the Greek Jews showed an interest in meeting Jesus, it was the need for complete and willing obedience which he stressed. Philosophical discussion and interest can serve as introductions to Jesus, but eventually we are challenged with the requirement to obey, with all the courage and trust that this involves. No longer can we follow Jesus when the mood takes us, or when we approve of the liturgy/music/homily. No longer can we excuse our need for regular times set aside each day for prayer and reading the Bible.

If we really want to follow Christ we have no choice but to become obedient, and lay our ambitions, plans and loyalties down at his feet. We may find that we are enabled to do this in one fell swoop. But however it happens, it will be done in a supportive and encouraging atmosphere, because God our Father is not a domineering slave-driver but a tender and caring parent who enjoys our company and wills for our salvation.

YEAR 2

JEREMIAH 31:31-34

Our Bibles are divided into the Old and New Testaments, and there is a very good reason for this. When Jesus offered the wine as the blood of the new covenant, he was saying that the prophesied new covenant between God and his people was now being made, through himself.

From now on the law would be written on people's hearts. When we share in Christ's dying we allow God to take over and be in charge of our lives. All the richness of com-munal worship and all the structuring of Christian care emanate from this kind of total, personal commitment to God.

HEBREWS 9:11-14

For Christ's sacrifice is so much more effective than any sacrifice of animals, which had to be offered time and again under the old Law in order to cleanse people of their sin. In contrast, Jesus offers himself, sinless as he is, to die as the punishment for our sins. That is why his death frees us from the effects of sin and liberates us from the prison of selfishness. We are now free to get on with living, in the rich, fulfilling, valuable way that God has planned for us to enjoy.

MARK 10:32-45

The wonderful thing about the Christian message is that we do not have to walk around with our faces set in a tight, determined smile. We are not to feel guilty about heartbroken sobs, the ache of missing our loved ones who have died, or the sense of abject misery that may wash over us in a seemingly endless illness. For the central event of Christ's life, the event that saves us, is the slow and lingering death by crucifixion. And we need to remember that Jesus was not anaesthetised. He felt it all. His loving Father allowed it to happen. That is how we know that the result of his suffering was astoundingly good.

It would be wrong to teach people that turning suffering into joy means taking away the pain. Sometimes this may happen, but at other times God allows the suffering to continue, just as he allowed the crucifixion to continue unchecked. But, just as that was the only way to resurrection and wholeness, so God will act through our suffering, if we let him, to enrich us, and bring about a transformation for great good.

Palm Sunday

Jesus enters Jerusalem as the Prince of Peace, riding on a donkey. At the heart of our rejoicing is the pain he is bound to suffer in redeeming us through unflinching love. Yet we still certainly rejoice, for we know he has won the victory. Jesus is indeed our King.

YEARS 1 AND 2

ISAIAH 50:4-9A

PHILIPPIANS 2:5-11

MARK 14:32-15:41

Through his own personal suffering and humiliation, the obedient servant in the Isaiah prophecy is able to teach others about the uncompromising love of God. In Jesus this song takes on a new and astounding reality, for here is the Son of God, with whom God is 'well pleased', undergoing insults, slander, torture, death, and, perhaps most hurtful of all, desertion by every one of his followers and even a sense of isolation from his Father.

However can such a bleak and distressing drama be cherished generation after generation? Why did God not answer Jesus' desperate prayer that the horror might be averted?

When Jesus returned to find the disciples sleeping, perhaps his words applied also to himself: 'The spirit is willing but the flesh is weak'. For here is the essence of what it meant to save us from the prison of sin; God had to empty himself of all rights, privilege and status and become utterly weak and vulnerable; he had to submit to the very worst that evil could throw at him and still continue to love, forgive and trust. Had his flesh not been weak he would not have been able to make this complete sacrifice; had his spirit not been willing, he would not have been able to achieve this ultimate in loving obedience.

Yet even at his most helpless, most cruelly treated and most terribly alone, Christ still loved the world which rejected him, and it is the incredible wonder of such love that draws us stumbling to his feet.

Maundy Thursday

The new Covenant between God and his people. The Passover feast was an annual celebration of God freeing his people from slavery. The blood of the lamb protected them, and was both a sacrifice and food before their journey. Now Christ offers himself in the bread and wine and in the washing of feet. His sacrifice frees us from sin's slavery.

YEARS 1 AND 2

EXODUS 12:1-14

The profound significance of this occasion is marked by the ritual and the reordering of the calendar. (Every time we write the date we have a similar reminder of God's great act of incarnation.)

The instructions are highly practical for a meal before a journey, and often the fulfilment of God's will depends on people obeying his instructions, however odd or irrelevant they may seem. For the chosen people, this sets them apart and protects them from the destroying plague in Egypt.

I CORINTHIANS 11:23-29

It is no accident that the Last Supper was a celebration of Passover. The symbolism would now be given new meaning, and the new covenant marks the next stage in God's relationship with his people.

And just as the people of Israel were instructed to celebrate Passover as a festival every year, so we are instructed to celebrate the Eucharist regularly until the second coming.

JOHN 13:1-15

There is only a thin dividing line between self- respect and arrogance. 'No self-respecting person would allow himself to be treated like that', we often hear, and we may instinctively shy away from being helped if we feel it is an insult to our independence or ability. Peter was offended by Jesus' behaviour: perhaps he felt that Jesus was degrading himself by doing a servant's job, and he wanted no part in it. It didn't seem right for a Lord and Master to be washing feet. How would we feel if a bishop came to the parish and started cleaning everyone's shoes!

Jesus again uses a physical act to explain the love he was telling them about. In the act of feet washing, in which they were involved, they could see that his love was not an emotional feeling or vague affection. It meant renouncing all right to rank and privileges, and serving reverently wherever there may be needs.

Those in need are not always the most attractive or pleasant people to deal with; they may smell, insult us, inject themselves with heroin or sleep around irresponsibly. They may encompass all the values we reject. But none of this matters, for we are not asked to like, or fall in love with one another – only to love one another. That involves the will, practical care, generosity and commitment. And we may well find that this leads to deeper, warmer friendships than we had believed possible.

Good Friday

Jesus lays down his life for us. He yearns so much for us to be saved that he undergoes death, allowing the burden of the whole world's evil to rest on his shoulders. Not once does he stop loving and forgiving. His death is no failure, then, but an accomplishment of cosmic proportions, through which we are saved.

YEARS 1 AND 2

ISAIAH 52:13-53 END

It is certainly amazing, and proof of God speaking through the prophets, that this passage strikes to the very core of how the world was to be saved. The idea of God's obedient servant being prepared to suffer and die in order to bring others to peace and understanding, is taken up and richly fulfilled by Jesus on the cross. The unthinkable insult – of the creator being destroyed by his created – has actually happened: God is being put to death while 'praying all the time for sinners'.

HEBREWS 10:1-25 OR HEBREWS 10:12-22
OR HEBREWS 4:14-16; 5:7-9

This act, more than any other, points to the end of our hopeless yearnings and desolate loneliness. God is not a distant and unapproachable ideal but a person – warmblooded and tactile, with pulse and breath. His loving is not a condescending 'playing' but a close relationship with deep affection and empathy. So much so, that he identifies completely with us in all our best moments and our most appalling ones. At the times we come, exhausted, to the end of our strength, and have nothing left to draw on, we find Jesus – not in the distance with his back to us, but right next to us, lifting us up to carry us to safer ground. His willingness to die the crucifixion death is our guarantee that he will never, ever desert us, and no suffering we face is beyond his reach;

always he suffers alongside us and leads us through it to new life.

JOHN 18:1-19:37 OR JOHN 19:1-37

Dare we pledge ourselves to Christ's way? When we read the account of his crucifixion the example it shows is so daunting. It is relatively easy to say 'use me, Lord' in the safety and fellowship of worship, and certainly this is the right beginning.

But we are bound, as indeed Jesus was, to recoil from the horrors of physical torture, emotional taunting and ridicule, or the call to submit obediently without gaining anyone's approval or praise. When we feel very much alone, and the God-given task weighs heavily and seems to be doing no one any immediate good; when we are tired and mocked for taking it seriously – these are the times we are truly offering ourselves for God's use. Such times must be expected and not resented, for they are the moments when we have the privilege of identifying with the suffering Christ. They are the times when others can be drawn to the strange freedom which owes nothing to comfort or a substantial bank balance, and everything to repentance, forgiveness and love.

Easter Day

Jesus is risen from the dead! Having passed through death to life, Christ has won the victory over everything evil and destructive. Full of glory and power, he enables us to bring the hope and joy of resurrection into the world's problems and tragedies. With God, nothing is impossible .

YEARS 1 AND 2

ISAIAH 12 OR EXODUS 14:15-22 OR ISAIAH 43:16-21

From the very beginning of matter God has been in charge. He chose to fashion the universe, and through his will and command it was created with all its potential for life and variety. Even as it was being formed, God's plans for its direction and purpose were fully developed. Gradually, through history we can see that plan unfolding, as a tentative, halting progress, often spoiled but repaired; often wounded but healed; often wandering but led back to the source of creation, by the creator himself who loves what he has made.

In these readings we see God's faithfulness and abiding love shown to his people. He has provided for them, saved them, comforted them and never forsaken them, in spite of all their waywardness and sin. Neither will he ever forsake us, for not only is he just, but he is also full of love, as we see for ourselves in Jesus Christ.

REVELATION 1:10-18 OR I CORINTHIANS 15:20 OR COLOSSIANS 3:1-11

Not only has Christ conquered death and sin by breaking through them to unending life. He has also brought us back to life lived in the way God planned when he created us. But there is no way we can half die with Christ if we are to be brought back to true life with him. It simply cannot be done, though often we pretend it can. We submit bits of ourselves but hang on to other bits with a grip of steel. Perhaps we are frightened we may lose our identity along with our companionable sins. Danger and insecurity yawn before us if we contemplate really radical changes in our giving and our life-style.

And we are right to count the cost first, for there is no doubt that there will certainly be risks and hardships. Living in Christ is rarely comfortable and never settled; it is full of the unexpected, of constant rethinking, challenge and change. It never allows us to get fixed in a rut or creep into holes when danger threatens.

But then, Christ never promised us a rose garden on the world's terms. We are to look instead for the heavenly things which belong with life in Christ. These treasures – such qualities as truth, joy, compassion and serenity – pour out in profusion, last through all affliction and satisfy as nothing material can. It is infinitely worth taking the risk, and giving ourselves away.

MATTHEW 28:1-10 OR JOHN 20:1-10 (OR 1-18)
OR MARK 16:1-8

As Creator, God has rested on the seventh day after accomplishing his work. Now, as Saviour, God keeps the Sabbath after the accomplishment of his redeeming work. With the beginning of a new week comes the most amazing new life which is forever free of the threat of death. Now Jesus emerges triumphant over humanity's fall from grace. The blockade is down, just as the stone has been rolled away, so that the way is now clear for us to be children of our heavenly Father, loving and beloved in a close relationship which death cannot destroy.

These very human, realistic accounts of Easter morning show us the lovable, varied characters and their predictable reactions to an unimaginably amazing event. We see Mary of Magdala, distressed at finding the physical body of Jesus missing; the petrified guards; the younger John racing ahead, but losing his nerve; the elderly Peter, puffing up behind and impetuously running straight into the tomb. We, too, all react differently and will have different experiences of the resurrection in our own lives.

The important thing is that they all suddenly realised what Jesus had meant about rising from the dead. It was not to be an other-worldly rising from which they were excluded: suddenly they understood that he meant real life – fulfilled, accomplished, physical and spiritual – a total existence. Not only had Jesus become man: he had also brought humanity into the very essence of the Godhead.

1st Sunday after Easter

The life-giving presence of the risen Lord. The disciples began to realise that Jesus was present with them whether they could see him or not. We, too, experience his spiritual presence among us and welcome him with joy.

YEAR 1

EXODUS 15:1-11

Moses and the people of Israel are jubilant because they have just been rescued from death. Such times make us acutely aware of the splendour of life! They burst into song to praise God who has shown himself in control as their loving parent, involving himself with their misery and intervening personally to save them.

I PETER 1:3-9

Peter's letter is very encouraging, particularly for any who are finding life difficult. He assures us that any patience or perseverance we practise during rough patches of our lives will be kept in heaven, and form part of the glory that will be revealed at the end of time.

It may look as if we are failures in the world's eyes; we may feel as if we are bashing our heads against a brick wall as we try to bring up our children as Christians in a materialistic and pagan world, hold an unstable marriage together, or cope positively with unemployment or illness.

It is how we respond to these challenges and trials which will make the lasting treasure. Instead of trying to act independently of God we can trust him and use his grace of forgiveness, his patience, his perseverance and his strength. The privilege of working with God like this takes much of the sting out of the suffering, and an incongruous joy wells up even among the tears.

JOHN 20:19-29

Thomas was not with the other disciples when they were joined by Jesus. It cannot have come as a surprise to Thomas that Jesus would be killed; he had expected it earlier when they returned to Bethany to visit Lazarus' grave. Thomas had been prepared to die with him. So if Thomas thought of Jesus as a great prophet, and a remarkable man, then he would have to sort out the rest of his life, trying his best to follow the example of his dead teacher. The prospect would be daunting in its loneliness.

He must have had niggling questions about those strange sayings of Jesus concerning new life, and rising again. Thomas was too dedicated to his human teacher to insult him by believing fairy stories – Jesus being alive again was simply too 'good' to be true: he preferred Jesus to be human and dead.

When he did meet the risen Christ, his amazed acclamation of faith shows what had happened. Thomas had swapped a human teacher for all-powerful God; Christ was not only to be loved and listened to, but actually worshipped. It is not idolatry for us to worship Christ, although he has a human face.

YEAR 2

EXODUS 16:2-15

The enthusiasm and excitement of the great escape from Egypt has started to wear off; and the people begin to feel their vulnerability and precarious survival out here in the wilderness, far from their familiar routine. Their panic leads them to grumble at Moses who stirred them up to go in the first place. So what God provides is not just food, which is the immediate problem, but also reassurance, which feeds a much more fundamental need of his children who are frightened and feel threatened. If we find ourselves nagging and grumbling, it may be worth laying aside all those things people are doing to irritate and make life difficult for us, and instead ask God to give us reassurance of his love. When he does so, we shall probably find that the urge to nag has disappeared!

And if in our parish there seems to be a lot of carping and petty-mindedness, it is often because the critics feel vulnerable and threatened in some way. Ministering to their fundamental need for reassurance of being loved, cherished and valued will promote deeper healing than head-on collisions over spiteful criticisms.

I CORINTHIANS 15:53-END

Underlying all our efforts to become more loving people, is the inspiring fact that God has intervened to save us from our own destructive nature by becoming man himself and gathering all that experience, including death, into the realm of eternity. Knowing this, we need not be downhearted, however badly things appear to be going, or however little we are appreciated. As Mother Julian of Norwich said: 'All shall be well, and all manner of things shall be well'.

JOHN 6:32-40

Christianity must never, in any circumstances, become an elitist or exclusive religion; and if we catch even a hint of it, red lights of warning should start flashing in our heads. When we read the words of Jesus it is quite clear that the good news of hope is freely available to all who believe, and no race or class is excluded.

Our spiritual feeding is provided to sustain us on our spiritual journey and we need it just as much as we need food for our bodies. It is also a source of great joy, because through it we experience the individual, personal love our heavenly Father has for each of us.

2nd Sunday after Easter

Jesus leads and teaches us his ways like a good shepherd. We recognise his voice and he knows each of us by name. Just as he led the disciples, on the road to Emmaus, to the point where they recognised him in the breaking of bread, so he leads us, his sheep, to know him and trust him.

YEAR 1

ISAIAH 25:6-9

The cross stands at the centre of the Bible: all the Old Testament looks towards it and all the growth of the Church is based on its foundation. The prophets had foretold that God would rescue his people, and, through them, the world. All through the years and generations the people looked forward to the coming of the Messiah, their understanding of what this meant gradually developing into the Saviour King whose reign would be established and grow for ever.

REVELATION 19:6-9

As Christ enters new life at the resurrection, heaven is seen here rejoicing that all the prophecies are fulfilled in a way which goes far beyond the reign of any earthly king, however fine and noble. This Kingdom breaks open the barriers between the physical and the spiritual, between time and eternity, between heaven and earth. It means that while still walking through life in the world, we can also live, think, see and move as citizens of heaven. Christ is our King, and his heaven can now be our 'territory'.

LUKE 24:13-35

The two disciples had been full of expectation. As Jesus' ministry progressed they had begun to see that he was not only a great prophet but possibly the Messiah himself. Now, at last, the Roman occupation would become a thing of the past, and Israel would once more be free and powerful.

The nails hammered into Jesus' body on Good Friday had hammered into their fervent hopes and dreams. No angel came to save him from death and when he died, so did their illusions.

Now Jesus approaches them, not abandoning them for having got it wrong, but working to redirect, explain and enlighten. Never mind if they didn't recognise him during the learning – they listened and began to think more openly, to broaden their expectations until, at the breaking of bread, things fell into place and they were filled with tremendous joy.

YEAR 2

EZEKIEL 34:7-16

Yahweh's character of active care and selfless compassion is being blocked by the very 'shepherds' who are supposed to be acting in his name. Their self-interest and carelessness has caused many to wander into danger and get lost.

The good shepherd will be personified in the person of Jesus, whose care, patient guidance and loving involvement has won the hearts of millions for nearly 2,000 years.

I PETER 5:1-11

Corruption can start anywhere. Nothing is immune, and certainly not the church, which is naturally enough a prime target for temptation. History can supply us with plenty of evidence that power corrupts, and as soon as any religious leadership forgets that the power and the glory belong to our heavenly Father, there are bound to be destructive and divisive 'shepherds' whose 'sheep' suffer and get led astray.

So we need to be constantly vigilant and rigorous with ourselves, re-committing ourselves regularly, examining our consciences and checking our priorities. We shall then be working in partnership with Christ and our lives, lived in his strength, will draw others to the joy of his love.

JOHN 10:7-16

Anyone who has walked along behind sheep will realise what Jesus meant when he talked so often of humans as sheep. They scuttle out of immediate danger and immediately start eating, as if nothing had happened. Seconds later they see danger catching up with them again so there is another short-lived scuttle, as they follow each other however foolishly they are led.

Hence the need for a really trustworthy shepherd, for sheep are woefully in need of a responsible leader. (Of course, the shepherds in Israel always lead, rather than drive the sheep, as in Britain.)

Some of those posing as the good shepherd can be very convincing, so that we sheep are sometimes coaxed into trusting them.

3rd Sunday after Easter

Jesus is the resurrection and the life. Not only does he live for ever –
he is actually life. When we put our trust in him, we become part
of that full, complete life, which death will not destroy.

YEAR 1

ISAIAH 61: 1-7

The prophet's message is about hope in hopeless situations;
restoration replacing decay; vigorous growth and vitality
springing out of ruin and desolation. Good news, indeed!

Does it seem too good? Can anything really have such
astonishing results? Is it perhaps all just wishful thinking?

The transformation may seem impossible, but time and
again God proves it to be real – both in individual lives and in
world events, whenever people abandon themselves to God. It
may not take place in a flash of magic, but its growth is strong
and gradual, just like renewal in nature. Think, for instance,
of the abolition of slavery, or the improvement of appalling
working conditions in the mines, or the present task of
enabling everyone to have access to fresh water.

In all dramatic social improvements, action does not
begin until people's hearts are open to see evil and burn to
overcome it with good. And it works. Working in tune with
the God of Life, we can bring life to every situation, however
depressing.

I CORINTHIANS 15:1-11

Paul's calling was radical and spectacular and he never loses
his amazement that God should choose one who had actually
persecuted his followers. But having accepted the call, he gets
on with the important business of spreading God's saving
truth, devoting his entire life and energy to it, and finding
that God's rich grace is always sufficient for all his needs.

JOHN 21:1-14

Even his close friends did not at first recognise Jesus. Perhaps their minds were still half-closed to the possibility of resurrection: they had even returned to the boats Jesus had called them from. But once they realise, there is no more doubt, even though the strangeness of it all frightens them.

As so often happens, a deeper knowledge of Jesus gives rise to a deeper responsibility. Peter, gently and deliberately forgiven for his denial, is commissioned as a shepherd, to look after the wayward and feed them. Jesus will never lead us forward so we can can bask in the sun and enjoy our private insights. He will always lead us in order to use us, so we should not be surprised, but honoured, if we find ourselves in situations which may be difficult. We are probably there for a reason: God has work for us to do.

YEAR 2

I KINGS 17:17-END

Having been fed and sustained by the widow, Elijah wrestles with what seems such cruel injustice. Surely God will not allow her son to die after she has shown such trust and kindness to the man of God.

Elijah pleads with God for the child's life, and his prayer is answered: the child lives, and the widow's faith is strengthened. Had Elijah not intervened, the child would surely have died. Sometimes it takes a state of desperation and heartbreaking anguish to get us praying – really praying – with our whole being. God never rejects such prayer. But, seeing life in terms of eternity, restoration to vitality may sometimes involve vitalising spiritual deadness, rather than physical, and therefore temporary health.

When we throw ourselves on his mercy in times of terrible need and despair, we can trust him absolutely to do what is best for us and the one we pray for.

COLOSSIANS 3:1-11

For in Christ we can at last stop pretending; stop inventing distractions to keep us from uncomfortable questions fearful of drowning in the conviction that, though materialism is all, it is entirely unsatisfying.

Christ is not just a set of ideas, but the living God with a human face who can show us what life is really about, and confirm our suspicions that the material world is not the reason for our existence.

He can help us break our dependency on the created world, until we have resumed our priorities. Then we begin to know the relief of centring our lives on something of real, ultimate value. This puts our whole existence in a new perspective and brings with it an inner peace and order.

JOHN 11:17-27

Overwhelming sadness and loss of a loved one comes through this account very powerfully. Jesus feels it, even though he knows that Lazarus will rise again. It is important that we feel able to mourn; squashing our human grief firmly out of sight in an effort to be brave can actually damage us emotionally and create long-term problems of adjustment. Yet at the same time, beneath the pain of grief, is the quiet reassurance that Jesus is here, Jesus loves, and Jesus cancels death.

When he raised Lazarus to life, all those who witnessed the event could see that God's care and love did not finish with the pulse, and was stronger than physical death. Even then not everyone believed. We are each of us shown evidence of God's love in action: whether we believe it or not is a personal decision which no one else can make for us.

4th Sunday after Easter

Jesus is the Way, the Truth and the Life. As we follow in his footsteps we experience the fellowship of his company, which gives us both courage to do his work and also peace of mind, even when life is difficult.

YEAR 1

ISAIAH 62:1-5

God's forgiveness is supremely generous; his loyalty is unswerving. He has promised to save his people and he will keep his word, so that they are uplifted and redeemed. Why will he do this? Simply because he loves his people.

REVELATION 3:14-END

We all do incredibly stupid and unkind things from time to time, not necessarily through malice but because we simply don't see at the time what damage our thoughtless words or actions are causing. In this passage the church in Laodicea is given a severe ticking off for such behaviour, which if we are honest with ourselves, we can see is a result of the kind of self-assured complacency which blinds us to the needs of others. When Mother Teresa visited London the press tried to draw her into describing the horrors of poverty in India. She shocked many people by talking instead about the spiritual poverty of many in the richer countries. It came as a surprise to many to find themselves described as being poor.

We don't have to be, of course. We can open the door when Jesus knocks, and enjoy the richness of his company for every day of our lives. It's just that so often we prefer the squalid, narrow darkness to the risk of opening up to the Lord of Light.

JOHN 21:15-22

God's forgiving nature and his yearning for us to be reconciled with him is illustrated clearly in this conversation between Jesus and Peter. We can all understand why Peter had denied Jesus – it's just the kind of thing that many of us would do in the circumstances – but that doesn't make it right, or even excusable. God never pretends we haven't sinned when we have; what he does is to encourage us to repentance and then offer his complete forgiveness. Then we can get on with our journey together, for the good of the world.

YEAR 2

PROVERBS 4:10-19

The image of a clear, well-lit path is a good one for describing the right way to 'walk' through life. It even sounds fairly straightforward, for we have all the signposts to tell us which way to go. But whether you are out rambling or driving through a one-way system in a strange town, the theory never seems to work out in practice. Signposts are rarely enough to stop you making several unintentional detours! Sound though the advice in this passage is, it highlights the rather disheartening human weakness of finding it virtually impossible to obey rules for long, however fine they may be.

II CORINTHIANS 4:13-5:5

In Jesus, however, freely given obedience is clearly visible. Even while on the receiving end of man's rejection, he submitted willingly to God's law of outreaching and forgiving love. In him the rejected God, and the man choosing to love, are fused together, producing such a highly potent force that evil can no longer win.

This would only be useful to us if we could in some way join forces with Jesus, this man/God; if only there were some way of soaking up his life-force, we could actually share the triumph over evil in our own lives!

Happily for us, that is exactly what God makes possible. The only credential needed is to believe in Jesus, and then we are given a free pass for the very qualities which seem so unattainable. We are promised new, rich, full lives, not just in this world but in the world to come, in the light of which, the alluring glitter and neon tempting us to sin, are shown up clearly for the sham and deceitful trash they are.

JOHN 14:1-11

So we can take heart and be encouraged, because Jesus does not just give us a list of instructions and directions – he actually comes with us every spiritual mile of the way. As we travel there will be conversation, which is prayer. As we watch how our companion deals with hostility, danger and weariness we shall learn through experience the good way to tackle problems, and we shall gradually become more and more like him. Then we will realise the joy of what it means to be truly a child of God – for our companion is both God's Son and our brother.

5th Sunday after Easter

Nothing can ever separate us from God's love. Our new life in the risen Christ is a journey home to the Father, and since God is on our side we need not be anxious and afraid, no matter what may happen to us on the way.

YEAR 1

HOSEA 6:1-6

On his side, God is utterly dependable. If he promises us something he will never go back on his word and he never reaches a point beyond which he loses interest in us or feels we are no longer worth bothering with.

In contrast, our love for him is often spasmodic and wavering, as ephemeral as clouds or morning dew. Since we are made in the likeness of God, we are actually capable of much deeper, stronger love, and do often give it to parents, marriage partners or close friends.

This is the kind of love God wants us to have for him, and for those he has made, rather than a casual habit of going through the motions of sacrifice (or, in our terms, church-going and prayer reciting).

I CORINTHIANS 15:21-28

It is impossible to explain eternal matters in terms of time, or to explain the relationship between Christ and the Father in human terms, since these things are more vast and extraordinary than we can ever understand. But Paul does his best, and through his earth-bound words we can glimpse something of the cosmic glory of God's plan surging into a splendid accomplishment, ordered and perfect, bearing along with it, as a huge glacier collects varied rocks and minerals, all sorts of different lives.

Death is the great barrier between time and timelessness and Christ has already broken through it. When all who belong to him in every age have been raised to life, death will itself have died, and the great work of an almighty, loving God will be complete in a perpetual state of joy, peace and love.

JOHN 16:25-END

Jesus is the first fruit and his was the loneliest journey ever made. We sense his human apprehension here, when he knows what is before him and knows, too, that even his most loyal friends will be unable to support him. Almost immediately comes the inner assurance from God, his Father, to encourage and strengthen him – Jesus will not be entirely alone because God will never desert him, even though he may be hidden from sight and insight. The tone of Jesus' words changes from sorrow to confident and inspiring joy as he remembers his Father's unswerving loyalty and love. It can sustain and encourage us as well, because the promise extends to everyone who puts trust in God.

YEAR 2

DEUTERONOMY 34

Moses' great spiritual journey home was matched with his leadership of the great desert journey of the people of Israel to their promised homeland. He is respected and honoured throughout Judaism, Christianity and Islam, and the overpowering mark of his greatness is his closeness to God all along the way.

ROMANS 8:28-END

When we are down on our luck, feeling at our worst and least pleasant or attractive, or needing the kind of help which involves using people's time and energy – these are the times we find out who our real friends are. Mysteriously, some 'friends' are nowhere around, while others (often those who surprise us) turn out to have accepted us, warts and all, and are prepared to put themselves out to help us.

God's love is of that steadfast, persevering and loyal kind, which means that we do not need to put on any mask in his company. He knows our bad tempers, irritating habits, personal indulgences and particular nastinesses, which we prefer not to be seen too often. He knows us at our very worst, and yet still loves us and tenderly cares for us, boots us sharply if we need it, gives us opportunity for rest when we are getting frayed at the edges, plunges us into hard work when we can cope and buoys us up on a calm sea of peace when everything around us is in turmoil.

That is the kind of love which binds us to Christ, and the bond is surer and firmer than any glue. Nothing can worm its way between us and not even the most terrible catastrophes affect it: not even death itself. He holds out his hand to us; if we take it, we shall never be lost or alone again.

JOHN 16:12-24
Jesus' teaching to his puzzled and rather bewildered disciples speaks of a constantly growing and developing relationship; our faith is not a pickled, presented entity but a dynamic, living organism, constant and yet flowing. We curb its flow and block its power whenever we forget this.

For Jesus is not only a historical figure living in Palestine during the Roman occupation there. He is also alive now and in every generation, speaking the language of each age and culture, understanding the particular problems and temptations of every time and nation.

So our faith is never outdated or irrelevant; provided we are receptive to God, he will always express himself in ways that humanity understands, and always lead us in truth.

Ascension Day & Sunday after Ascension

Jesus has ascended into heaven. With his ministry complete, and death conquered, Jesus takes his place at the right hand of God. No longer tied by time and place he reigns in glory.

YEAR 1

DANIEL 7:9-14

This amazing vision looks through the darkness of time to the joy of heaven, as Jesus is led into God's presence, having accomplished the saving of humankind. Of course, no pictures can really grasp the meaning, but Daniel's language gives us a wonderful sensation of worth, dignity, grace, truth and rejoicing. Like a magnet, Christ draws many people from all nations into his kingdom which shall never end.

We have the privilege of living in this last age, when all the peoples of the earth are being brought to know and acknowledge him as Lord of All.

EPHESIANS 1:15-END

When we look at the incredible details of Jesus' life – his teaching and signs, his death and resurrection – we cannot fail to be impressed, by the power illustrated there. Thankfully it is a loving power; some of the 'star wars' sagas hint at the terror and devastation that would result from a similarly powerful force of evil. Though fiction, all such stories, both ancient and modern, depict an instinctive human terror of evil taken to the ultimate.

As Christians we are privileged to see glimpses of goodness taken to the ultimate. It is revealed in the person of Jesus, who, through complete unselfishness, has brought mankind into a new relationship with the seat of power – God himself.

His great, universal, cosmic presence draws all things towards the splendid all-glorious harmony of completion. We have been chosen to work in harness with him to achieve it.

LUKE 24:45-END

Jesus emphasises the fact that his death and suffering were all a necessary part of his work of salvation. Without his physical presence which they have always relied on, the disciples needed to understand the mystery of how death is a source of life, suffering a source of joy, and giving a means of receiving. They cannot understand these things without Jesus, so he promises them his ever-present life – his Spirit; and the disciples, trusting him, return to Jerusalem full of joy.

YEAR 2

2 KINGS 2:1-15

To be allowed to see Elijah taken up into heaven meant that Elisha would indeed be granted his request – to inherit a double share of Elijah's spirit. We can see the parallels between this account and the account of the disciples who witnessed Jesus' ascension and also received his spirit.

Such insight and perception was only possible because both Elisha and the disciples made themselves available, and were used to seeing God working in the master they followed. Elijah, following in the great tradition of Moses, had been drawn to an intimate relationship with God; it was these two who spoke with Christ at the Transfiguration, which three of the disciples also witnessed. Their lives express the powerful and dramatic use God makes of lives which are freely offered for his service.

EPHESIANS 4:1-13

After the Ascension, Jesus will no longer be with his disciples; he will be in them instead, and they prepare themselves to receive his power.

The power they await is unmatched by any other power in any generation. Its potency brought stars and planets into being, generates life, and charges the universe with purpose; in Christ it broke through death and destruction to unsurpassed glory. All time and space is poised in the harmony of that power; and as limbs and organs of Christ's Body, the Church, we have it pulsing through us, vital and glowing. Through us Jesus reaches everyone we talk to, everyone whose lives our lives touch. Through us he restores confidence, soothes and comforts, strengthens and supports, heals and reconciles. Whenever we decide not to co-operate, the whole Body's effectiveness is weakened.

Luke 24:45-end

As witnesses to Christ's ascension, his disciples are commissioned to tell the Good News in Christ's name to all the nations, starting where they are already – Jerusalem. It was a commission which could only come from one who was divine, with full authority over everything, seen and invisible. In his body, Jesus ministered to those living in and around Galilee; in his spiritual body (which includes us) he would be ministering to every person in every country. That is what mission is all about.

We may not need to travel very far before we meet people who do not yet know Jesus. They may be lost, or searching among the dustbins for spiritual food, when there is a meal served up specially for them. It is both our duty and our joy to bring these people to Christ; to introduce them to Christ by our caring behaviour, our forgiveness, open-heartedness and joy.

Pentecost

The Holy Spirit, poured out on the disciples with a rush of wind and with tongues of fire. Ever since, God's Holy Spirit has enriched and empowered all who open their hearts and minds to receive.

YEARS 1 AND 2

GENESIS 11:1-9

This is not a cautionary tale against progress; it is a story which illustrates humanity's mistake in attempting to 'outdo' God and live independently from him. The ziggurat on which the story is probably based, was an attempt to build a kind of holy mountain artificially in the middle of a flat plain. As we know from Moses and Elijah, mountains were considered special meeting places for God and his chosen; in that context we can appreciate the arrogance and insulting vanity of using the gift of unity for such a project.

or

EXODUS 19:16-25

When Moses leads the people of Israel to meet their God, the whole atmosphere is filled with awe and dread, highlighted by the quaking, fiery mountain, the sound of thunder and the smoke. Moses alone is summoned to the sacred top of the mountain to speak with God.

ACTS 2

The first effect of the Holy Spirit at Pentecost is the breaking down of barriers. All those present are able to understand the ecstatic message of God's saving power and love, unleashed as the Church is born. It is like the first fruits of a great harvest which still goes on today; it challenges the world with a radically new law of love; it is the victorious Christ, alive, strong and in charge. No wonder the disciples were full of such rapturous joy – if God was with them to this extent, then who could possibly be against them?

When we know this experience it is indeed breathtaking, invigorating and tremendously exciting. God has overcome the world. He comes with us in person.

ACTS 2:1-21

The apostles have been commissioned to tell all people everywhere about Jesus; the magnificent sign of being understood by everyone without a language barrier serves to encapsulate this task of the apostles and all their successors.

As time passes initial fervour usually fades, but since this fervour is occasioned by the power of a living God, it continues to burst out in every generation of believers. People still find their lives drastically transformed through an encounter with Christ; many still find the Spirit so real and invigorating that sacrifices are undertaken with joyful serenity; unpleasant and dangerous work is gladly undertaken; individuals stand firm to witness in a corrupt society, and countless numbers spread love and peace daily among those around them.

There is still much to be done. But, living in the Spirit, we can work as harvesters and take part in establishing God's kingdom on earth.

JOHN 14:15-26

Wherever people come together to focus their hope on their Lord, and submerge their own selfishness in their longing to be part of him, Jesus stands among them and his presence is powerfully experienced in a wave of joy. Although at such times Christians are aware of their unworthiness, Christ's presence does not give rise to an inward groan of despair as one might expect when he is so loving and we have let him down so often.

Instead there is a sense of contentment and tranquillity; a light-heartedness as all problems are seen in the context of someone who is loving, forgiving, and in full control. Faces relax and eyes soften; many feel great warmth of affection for those around them; many feel very close to loved ones who have died, as if the barrier of death is no longer there.

Such cherished times bind Christians together in the life of our Lord, and it is from such experiences of a real presence that all mission must spring. With the peace of God in us (which is, as Paul knew, quite beyond reasoned understanding) we shall be literally 'inspired' or 'breathed into' by the life of Jesus, so that we shall be able to bring him to each room we visit and each person we meet.

or

JOHN 20:19-23

The whole purpose of receiving the Spirit, then, is to use it. We are sent out in the Spirit's power to tell others that God loves them in a way they have always longed to be loved: loyally, honestly, uncompromisingly and tenderly. We are to invite others to come and meet Jesus for themselves; to introduce them to him both through our attitudes to people and events, and also by suggesting passages in the Bible to read, praying with them and telling them what Christ means to us and how he has changed our lives.

It is all too easy to assume everyone knows where to come and what to read if they are interested; but we cannot make any such assumptions. There is widespread ignorance today about the good news that means so much to us, and we are commissioned to make sure the news is spread. We never need worry about what words to use; if we live in the Spirit he will give us the best ones.

Trinity Sunday

The God we worship is Father, Son and Holy Spirit. The qualities of God are revealed in the three persons of the Trinity, and in us, too, when we found our lives on him. Filled with his life, the Christian community will be enabled to show the love of God, the grace of Jesus and the fellowship of the Holy Spirit.

Years 1 and 2

Isaiah 6:1-8

When the prophet sees a vision of God's glory, it brings home to him the shame of man's mean response to God and his corrupt hypocritical life, so empty and pompous.

God shows that he has power to forgive, so that the situation is not as hopeless as it seems. Having experienced the generosity of this forgiveness, the prophet is ready to offer himself as God's messenger.

Ephesians 1:3-14

When you walk up a hill or a mountain, you often head for 'false' summits on the way. They look like the top, but when you reach them you find the real summit is higher than you thought.

Imagining God's power, influence and control is a bit like that: however much understanding and awareness we grasp, there is always more than we can comprehend. But within it is the firm and dependable promise of Christ: that we have been chosen right from the beginning, and stamped with the seal of the Holy Spirit, to be freed sons and daughters of the God whose majesty is beyond us.

John 14:8-17

The most profound way in which God's nature is shown to us is in Jesus of Nazareth, the carpenter turned itinerant preacher, who slept, ate, got tired, knew fear and understood failure. This fully human being was, in some way that is impossible to explain in human terms, also God. In him mankind could see the nature of God expressed through voice, tears, healing hands, and dusty, travel-worn feet. Never before had God's qualities of tenderness and compassion, patience, kindness and faithfulness been so clearly seen.

Having seen Jesus we can understand more of God, and by believing, or putting our trust in him instead of ourselves or man-made commodities, we can be saved and liberated. We can also turn a blind eye to God's offer, and reject it and all the hope it contains. The choice is ours.

2nd Sunday after Pentecost

God's people are called to be united in the fellowship of the Spirit, sharing God's life. But we are given free will, so we can choose whether to be part of God's people or not.

YEAR 1

EXODUS 19:1-6

The people of Israel were chosen for a very important mission: their whole nation was to be a light shining in heathen darkness so as to draw the world to acknowledge God as Lord of all. To do this, their unity was crucial; they had to be a people obviously set apart from the cults and religions around them. Hence the binding covenant, demanding strong allegiance on both sides.

1 PETER 2:1-10

Peter explains the role of Christ's followers in terms of the children of Israel who were the chosen race, set apart for God's purpose. Then, the temple containing the ark of the covenant represented the dwelling place of the Almighty. Now that God has revealed himself in the person of Jesus, the temple housing his presence is built of living stones – the followers of Christ. By grace they have become the chosen race, which is no longer bound to any ethnic group but has widened to embrace those from all nations who acknowledge Jesus as Lord.

There are times when it comes as a nasty shock to find that people, whom perhaps we love dearly, are stumbling over the very rock which provides our own foundation. It can be very tempting to try to kick that rock away, for it seems to stand in the way of a precious relationship.

Of course, it cannot be discarded, for Jesus is the vital centre of salvation, without whom there is no hope or life or healing. Instead, we are to offer ourselves as a sacrifice so that through our lives being grounded in Christ, even the most cynical, the most unexpected, are drawn to experience the security and joy of living in Jesus.

JOHN 15:1-5

Jesus is quite clear and definite: if we do not live in him as closely as a branch lives on a vine, we shall bear no fruit at all. Not even the occasional grape! If you visit a vineyard, look closely at any succulent cluster of fruit and trace its stem. It may be trained some distance from the main branch, but eventually it joins the true vine with its strong root system (never a weak sucker shoot).

That is how we, too, will bear fruit – fruit in great clusters, like the grapes. But before we can flourish we shall need to be pruned, as any gardener knows. Any side shoots of distractions or weakening habits and sins need to be cut out, so that all our growth and energy are concentrated along the main fruiting branch. We may well dislike this pruning, and not recognise that it proves God's love for us. It can be useful, sometimes, to look again at some disappointment or failure we resent, and see if we can discern in it something that perhaps we needed to learn the hard way; or perhaps it may be the very thing to spur us into action from which great good will come.

YEAR 2

2 SAMUEL 7:4-16

The ark of the covenant was a symbol of God's constant presence among his people. He had heard their cries of anguish in Egypt and led them across the Red Sea to freedom; he had supported and guided them throughout their wandering years in the wilderness, and kept faith with them through their grumbles and idolatry. Now, for a while, King

David had established peace, and had the leisure to start plans for a permanent building to house the ark.

At first sight it seems to be a very good idea; noble, generous and necessary. But Nathan, being a man of God, mulls it over during the night and begins to see things in God's way. Perhaps a permanent house for the ark would destroy some very powerful symbolism: God is not anchored to one spot, but travels with us in times of danger, failure and victory; God is there among his people where they need him, and he will never abandon them.

In God's eyes the time is not yet right for such an enterprise, but he reaffirms his promise which spans a far broader plan even than building a magnificent temple: from the family of David will come one who displays God's eternal glory to the whole world.

We, too, need to be wary of planning ambitious works for God. They may not always be what he has in mind, or the timing may be wrong. We would be better advised to ask him first!

ACTS 2:37-END

Peter's witness to the resurrection of Jesus is unequivocal and full of conviction, for he has actually seen Christ alive after his crucifixion, and has even eaten and drunk with him. You don't eat and drink with an allegorical character or a vision. There is no doubt about what Peter is saying: Jesus' new life is real and complete. So to believe in Jesus as the living Lord is not something for the gullible and naive, since they are the only ones crazy enough to believe such an impossible tale. The belief is based on the evidence of hard-headed, working men who had themselves taken quite a lot of convincing. Of course it is impossible in purely human terms. That does not mean we need to remould the facts to fit human possibility; it means that we need to acknowledge that God is altogether 'bigger' that the human experience. We are not God – he is.

LUKE 14:15-24

Such teaching is shown in this parable of the invited guests who do not realise the importance of the invitation, and the rabble of poor and crippled who are enjoined to take their place at the dinner instead of those originally invited. At one level, Jesus was addressing the pompous and hypocritical religious leaders of his time, who considered their own petty affairs more important than the kingdom of heaven. At another level he speaks across the centuries of the longing God has to share a meal and fellowship with all his children gathered about him.

3rd Sunday after Pentecost

Through Christ we die to sin and are raised to full life. Jesus, the Christ, the Son of God, is the fulfilment of the prophecies and the only way to salvation.

YEAR 1

DEUTERONOMY 6:17-END

In our age of constant change the pressure is often on to discard the traditions of the past as being irrelevant. Such an attitude is shortsighted and arrogant, for we progress (or regress) as a society as well as in our individual lives.

Here we see the foundation of God's law being passed on from generation to generation so that the whole people can grow and develop as God's people.

ROMANS 6:3-11

The symbolism of baptism is easier to understand in total immersion, as early Christians would have known it. Wading into water and then being ducked right under it is a powerful reminder of drowning. Anyone who has seen the possibility of immediate death, whether by accident or illness, receding, will know the fresh clarity and thankfulness with which life is suddenly seen. Bird songs seem more lovely than ever, colours brighter, nature full of miracles and the privilege of being alive so great that one feels one will never grumble again.

Dying to sin and being alive to Christ is just like this; it creates a state of fresh joy and wonder at all that is hopeful, unobtrusively persevering, beautiful or touchingly honest. For it is the relief and heightened awareness that comes from being released from the condemned cell and told that we can go free. That is what resurrection means, and that is why it can be brought with powerful effect into every situation: having found ourselves set free we shall have a different outlook, and that will bring new hope to all areas, no matter how wearying and despairing they may seem.

JOHN 15:5-11

This passage really deals with getting things in proportion, and having our priorities right. When we love God first, our love for others increases by leaps and bounds: we may even find ourselves loving those we couldn't stand before. Our love for God may lead us to see areas of our character which needed to be changed, subdued, curbed or developed in order that we can be more loving; and because we love God we shall be willing to have a go at what he suggests, even if it is a bit humiliating and demands stepping down from a position proudly defended before. It may be only the equivalent of a cup of cold water that we give, but it will serve to increase our love both for God and for the recipient.

On the other hand, if our loving gets trapped in one area – either for a person or a thing – it will not be able to spread and grow in the same way since it is not rooted into the source of all love. It is likely, instead, to become possessive, narrow and exclusive. It must be defended against anyone threatening it, and if it lets us down (as may well happen) our world will seem devastated, for our ground of being will have been devastated.

That is why Jesus urges his followers to give their full allegiance to Love itself: all the rest, and more, will follow us all the days of our life, both here and in eternity.

YEAR 2

DEUTERONOMY 8:11-END

Even people who do not normally pray will fall on their knees when there is terrible danger or suffering. Often it is times of vulnerability that jerk us back to recognising our dependence on God. Yet so often, when everything is going really well, we forget to thank God, or even acknowledge that he has anything to do with 'our' success. Today's reading reminds us that we belong to God all the time, and must not forget him just because we are living in comfort – such times are opportunities for thanks and praise. Otherwise, we are really making gods of the things that surround us in our comfort.

ACTS 4:8-12

Peter and John are being embarrassing. They keep talking about Jesus of Nazareth as if he were still alive, even though everyone knows he has been put to death. The priests and elders just wish they would keep their fanciful, threatening ideas to themselves and let life go on in the comfortable, established way it always has done.

Unfortunately there is this tiresome cripple standing up in front of the people, large as life and twice as healthy; in fact, perfectly healed. Obviously some power must have been at work.

Why were they unable to accept the joyful truth of the resurrection on the evidence of such 'fruit'? Surely because they knew that acceptance would utterly change their lives (as it did in Paul's case, of course), and having put a lot into establishing their life-style, they reckoned they had too much to lose. Whereas the cripple, whose life had been held physically tight and rigid by his handicap, was wildly delighted at the flexibility and capacity for movement that God had now given him.

Two things, then, about the resurrection life: it shows, and it liberates; but not everyone wants to be liberated. Perhaps some area of our own life-style is causing us to hobble, spiritually. If so, the risen Jesus has the power and the desire to set us leaping!

LUKE 8:41-END

If we were to read the creation poem in Genesis, and then imagine how the God revealed there might react to a young girl desperately sick and dying, we would surely come up with the way Jesus feels deep sorrow, confronts the evil, overrules it with his authority of intense goodness, and creates an atmosphere of joy and wholeness.

Even though he is delayed by another act of healing (which remade the timid woman who had suffered for years), Jesus' power to make whole is not diminished. For Jesus it is never too late to bother; never too late to transform, heal and make whole. The wholeness may be different from what we were expecting, but God knows and loves us in terms of eternity, and will make us, and our loved one for whom we pray, healed in the way which is eternally best for us. We need to touch him with faith, invite him into the home or hospital, and listen to his instructions. He will never refuse to come.

4th Sunday after Pentecost

The freedom of the children of God which liberates them to serve others. Whenever we deny God through our words or actions it hurts him, because he longs for us to know the freedom and joy of serving him. When we speak and act as his friends there is great joy both for us and in heaven.

YEAR 1

DEUTERONOMY 7:6-11

It is very humbling to realise that we are going to church, I am writing this book and others are using it, not because we have chosen to but because God has chosen us. He actually likes our company so much that he has called us all to spend our lives with him!

We are, by adoption and grace, God's children. Not that we are worthy of it; we constantly let him down and allow selfishness to block his power. But if, every time we fall, we are sorry and become reconciled to him, God will bless us and use us in spite of (and even because of) our unworthiness. For he loves us with warmth and affection.

GALATIANS 3:23-4:7

Paul is stressing here the new-found unity which is a direct result of belonging to Christ. Baptism is like a kind of dying, in that it is a complete break with the world's categorising, compartmentalised society, divisive by its very nature .

New life in Christ is not the old with a few 'extras' thrown in; it is a complete remaking – more like a caterpillar's transformation into a butterfly .

We are often happiest with things as they are, reluctant to alter what we know and understand, even if there are difficulties. Yet we must risk ourselves with Christ if he is to change us.

JOHN 15:12-17

The transforming power is Love, personified in Jesus, who was prepared to expend his complete life in the service of others. He did not do this sourly, with a self-righteous expression and meaningful glances. He simply lost himself in loving and caring for any who needed his help, wanted to talk to him, or sought his company. He never gave the impression of being too busy for anyone, never missed an opportunity to encourage, sympathise or share a celebration. No genuine enquirer was ever made to feel small or inadequate. No one was made to feel excluded, no matter what kind of life they were leading. And the resultant changed and radiant lives were astounding. They still are.

YEAR 2

ISAIAH 63:7-14

The people of Israel, being human, did not remain true to their covenant, and there were many times when they hurt, angered and insulted their God by their rebellion and disloyalty. Like a human parent, God is seen here as feeling with them through all their sufferings and hardships, and loving them even in their spitefulness and nastiness. Not that God is blind to their faults: he knows just how mean and nasty they, and we, can be, but he loves us all the same.

ACTS 8:26-38

Philip, standing ready and available before the Lord, is therefore able to be used by him just when he is needed. Here was an enquiring, seeking person and through Philip God explained things and brought him to the joy of faith. No doubt the Ethiopian would have then spread the Good News further still.

    We, too, need to keep ourselves available for God's use; his life and power is given to us so that we can bring others to share in the freedom of God, so we must never hoard it, or keep it only for those we choose to help. Living in Christ's love means doing things his way, even if his choice of work for us comes as a surprise.

LUKE 15:1-10

Those who followed the Law worked hard at keeping God's word. They could see others flagrantly flouting his authority and disobeying the sacred commandments. No wonder it surprised and upset them to see Jesus mingling with those whom the Law condemned. It may not all have been jealousy: some may well have been seriously concerned that it might damage the moral and spiritual values of the most high God.

In none of these parables does Jesus condemn the scribes and Pharisees or praise the sinners. He simply shows those within the Law that there is a good reason for becoming involved with anyone who has gone the wrong way: caring involvement is the only way to bring them back.

This, of course, presented the religious leaders with a challenge, as it challenges all committed Christians. Do we love God enough to get involved with the hurt, diseased, embezzling, crooked, perverted and cruel? If we don't, then however are they to be made whole?

5th Sunday after Pentecost

God's Law, summed up in love. It is this law which undergirds us as we work with Christ to draw all people to the creator, by whom and for whom we were made.

YEAR 1

EXODUS 20:1-17

If we are to get the full impact of Jesus' teaching, we need to be familiar with God's Law as revealed to Moses. Although not the whole story, the commandments are still worth learning off by heart, however old-fashioned rote learning may be. Jesus certainly used them as the framework of his code of living.

The commandments are a God-given structure of right attitudes and behaviour, based firstly on placing God at the centre of life, and secondly on love and consideration for others. They may look negative with all those 'You shall not's' around, but if we look at them in the light of Jesus' summary of them, we can see that breaking any of the commandments involves a lack of caring love towards God and our fellow humans.

EPHESIANS 5:1-10

The light Christ brings into our lives is really 'enlightenment' for it means that, in his presence, right and wrong become clearer, and we can see how to act for good rather than evil.

One of the most alarming things about evil is that quite often we have simply no idea how destructive our well-meant behaviour can be. Without Christ it is not at all obvious and we desperately need his guidance, his light, to show up the areas of our characters which may seem all right to us, but which are causing others distress or blocking God's work. If we really want God to work in us then we must earnestly pray for his light. When it shines we can be sure of one thing – we shall not like what it shows at all, as it will be bound to touch raw nerves. We must pray bravely, then, in the knowledge that, even if it hurts to be put right, we shall be stronger, more useful Christians once God has been let in to heal.

MATTHEW 19:16-26

The danger of following rules in life is that we can feel that once we have completed our rules we have done all that is required. (It is this attitude, too, which is for ever totting up how many hours we are working and converting it into money earned, rather than doing a job cheerfully, just because it needs doing.)

The young man obviously felt dissatisfied with rule-following, but was not yet prepared for what Jesus suggested to him; Jesus' call had strings attached. Following Jesus will mean abandoning his wealth, and that is something the young man finds too hard.

Isn't this often true for us as well? We offer our day for Christ to use, and then when he accepts our offer and gives us some unpleasant job instead of what we had planned, we moan about what a tiresome day it has been! Our 'wealth' may be our time, energy, plans, and comforts, our routine, favourite programme, relaxing company or even the biscuits we were saving. And God asks us to be prepared to give them all away joyfully in his service.

YEAR 2

RUTH 1:8-17,22

This touching story of loyalty is a wonderful example of the kind of caring love which the God of love inspires. Ruth is not one of God's chosen people by birth, for she is a foreigner, but great good was to come through her, for she became the mother of King David's grandfather.

ACTS 11:4-18

Peter, who had been in Jesus' company from the start, still found it hard to accept that the Gospel was also for non-Jews. He was finally convinced through prayer, as a result of which he was given fresh insight. He then had to come to terms with the fact that he had been wrong before. But Peter does not wallow in embarrassment. As soon as he realises God's will he sets off to put things right, plunging straight into a new course of action. That shows real love for his Saviour; above his pride and his reasoned arguments for keeping Christianity Jewish, is set whatever Jesus wants to be done. If Jesus wants to include gentiles just as they are, then that is fine by Peter – he wants it too; even if it means changing his mind.

Whenever there is disagreement or heated discussion about any issue, we need to take a leaf out of Peter's book. First, setting ourselves to find out God's will by seriously asking him with prayer and fasting; and then, when we are receptive, recognising his will and acting on it, whether we agree with it or not. Obedience to God's will is what proves the extent of our love for him.

LUKE 10:1-12

This sending out of the seventy-two in pairs to preach repentance, and to heal, would have been in some sense a practice run for their commission after Pentecost. It would also have spread the news of the imminence of God's kingdom being established on earth. Jesus' instructions to them, as to us, are clear, practical and uncomplicated.

The point is not that we should all leave our families and set off without sandals or any spare clothes; rather, we need to spend time in the quietness of Christ's presence to listen to the instructions he has for us!

6th Sunday after Pentecost

In Christ we become a new person. As soon as we turn to approach God, he comes to welcome us; he accepts us just as we are and begins to heal our personalities, increase our capacity to love and to forgive, and enable us to become fully ourselves.

YEAR 1

EXODUS 24:3-11

A shared meal was one way of sealing a covenant between two parties, and here the leaders and elders of Israel share a meal in a literal 'summit' meeting. God is present among them in a very powerful way. They can sense the close bond with him at a time when their wills and hearts are fresh with zeal for keeping his Word. Like a prefiguring of Communion, God and his people eat and drink together in love and fellowship.

Blood, too, symbolic of life, was used in the sealing of a covenant. We can see here the leaning towards Christ's sacrifice, in which, through his spilt blood, we are brought back into fellowship with God.

COLOSSIANS 3:12-17

'Wearing' kindness, compassion and humility is quite different from carrying them around. Once on, clothes go everywhere we go, and unless they are definitely unsuitable for our activity we tend to forget about them and concentrate on what we are doing. Having chosen overalls to wear, we can paint the window frames without worrying about accidental spills; having chosen a raincoat and wellies we can take the children to school without moaning about getting wet. In other words, if we choose to wear suitable clothes, our attitudes and outlooks alter.

These qualities of compassionate caring are suitable clothes to wear for living a Christian life. If we mentally put them on when we dress each morning, we shall find them helping us through the day. It will not be an introverted obsession with how our 'clothes' look, but a practical confidence which enables us to fling ourselves whole-heartedly into the business of Christian caring without worrying about any possible damage to us. For these fruits are the loving Spirit of Christ living in us, and they equip us for the task of establishing and forging loving relationships, and making reconciliation a priority .

LUKE 15:11-END

It is a great relief to find that Jesus teaches, through this parable, that we can be accepted and saved even when we have made a thorough mess of our lives! There is no sin we may have committed which God will not forgive. Nothing we do will ever make us unlovable to God, our heavenly Father, and he will come running out to meet us even while we are still miles off.

If we feel sorry for the elder brother, we must remember the circumstances in which Jesus told his parable. The Pharisees and scribes were not wicked men. They had remained faithful through the centuries of history and obeyed the Law minutely. Similarly the elder brother had remained as a good and trustworthy member of his father's house. The trouble is that in our human weakness, we tend to become jealous of our positions, and instead of being delighted when newcomers discover what we have known for years, we are tempted to stand on what we feel are our privileges and rights.

Living in Christ turns this upside down. For if what we delight in is a state in which all men are reconciled to God in one great Kingdom of love, then, when others accept Christ, we will be so thrilled that we'll be feasting and welcoming for all we're worth!

'Thy Kingdom come', we pray. Do we really want the Kingdom of God enough?

YEAR 2

MICAH 6:1-8

In this passage we feel the heartache and sorrow of God which is personified in the anguish of Christ on the cross. So blind, so obstinate and so perverse is humanity that we are forever getting our priorities wrong, and racing at top speed in the wrong direction. Whenever our heads are down, concentrating on immediate satisfaction and self-centred reward, we lose sight of what we are created for. Then even our worship will become hollow and meaningless, and whatever we outwardly 'do' for God will mean nothing if it does not first spring from a thankful and loving heart.

EPHESIANS 4:17-END

Those who love are bound to get hurt sometimes. Those who love deeply may get badly hurt. And all our loving is only a faint reflection of God's love for us, so every time we turn our backs on what is right, indulge our spitefulness, cause friction or sulk, we reject the one who loves us completely. Anyone who has ever been rejected or slighted will know how much that hurts.

So our sin, our selfishness, causes the Holy Spirit of God to grieve; it fills him with great sorrow and hurts him deeply, in a personal way. And similarly he is personally delighted when we reflect his nature by being responsive, warm and loving people.

MARK 10:46-END

We do not know what made Bartimaeus blind, but when we meet him he strikes us as loudmouthed, bitter and aggressive. He certainly antagonises some of the crowd, who tell him to be quiet. His cry sounds hard, and full of unresolved resentment at his condition. He demands that everyone should feel sorry for him, for he feels so sorry for himself.

We might expect Jesus to go running over to see him straight away and put things right by making him see. But Jesus understands that the blindness is only part of the problem; healing will only happen to Bartimaeus' personality when he starts to reach out from himself and humble his heart to admit his need and ask for help, instead of nursing his self pity. (In treatment for addiction, healing begins when the addiction is admitted and the need for help acknowledged.)

Jesus sends instructions for the man to make the first move and approach him, and at the invitation Bartimaeus jumps up – he even flings off his cloak in his excitement. When he gets to Jesus there is a significant silence before Jesus prompts him to express his need. It comes out in a new, reverent and respectful manner, straightforward, and simply put. This changed attitude is an important part of the healing; his raw, desperate longing is fulfilled as he receives both sight and self respect.

7th Sunday after Pentecost

Love – the more excellent way of living. God is love, so when we live in love we live in God and he lives in us. In fact, every loving, caring and forgiving act is evidence of God's presence.

YEAR 1

HOSEA 11: 1-9

In spite of his people's waywardness and lack of fidelity, God loves them with tender, unswerving affection, and whenever they stray he labours to bring them back.

The Northern kingdom was fast approaching the threat of collapse after generations of unfaithfulness, self-indulgence and decadence. As the prophet Amos had pointed out, they deserved all they were going to get, for they had rejected God utterly, and God would be quite justified in abandoning them to their fate. But Hosea, personally wounded by his own beloved but unfaithful wife, was able to balance the justice of God's character with his tender mercy and forgiving love, and though deeply hurt and grieved by them, he is always willing to start afresh with them and welcome them back.

I CORINTHIANS 12:27-13 END

This most beautiful passage on Christian love is worth reading every day this week. It is so different from the world's values, and reaches to the heart of all Christ's life and teaching.

If we try putting our own name instead of 'love', we shall very quickly see how mean and lacking in love our lives often are.

But there is plenty of hope; by God's grace there are times when we do reveal these qualities, and so often these are the times we feel, surprisingly, not burdened by their weight, but refreshed and full of joy. The way of love is not heavy and oppressive at all – it actually brings the very peace and freedom that selfishness tries desperately to buy. God gives it to us, hands it out for free: can we afford not to accept it?

MATTHEW 18:21-END

When we hear this story, we probably share the indignation of the fellow servants at such injustice. The issue is clear and easily seen.

Unfortunately, in real life things are rarely so glaringly black and white, and it is quite possible for us to find we have been behaving like the unforgiving servant without even realising it. Often, it happens when we are under pressure, if: we have a deadline to meet, we shall probably take out our anxiety on those who hold us up; if money is scarce, we are more likely to flare up at anyone causing expensive damage.

Yet, when you think about it, such pressure is really caused by us keeping a tight grip on our lives instead of giving them away to Christ. If, when we feel the tension, we take a deep breath and remember that, as children of eternity, our lives are now spaces for God to work in, then the irritations and setbacks become opportunities to grow in patience, to spread God's kind of peace which the world lacks, and to put into practice his loving forgiveness.

YEAR 2

DEUTERONOMY 10:12-11:1

Although some of the scribes and Pharisees had made the Law very narrow and negative by Jesus' day, we can see here that it is really a broad, unprejudiced, positive attitude which is at the heart of the Law. Jesus, interpreting it as love for God and neighbour, was going right back to the fundamental values of loving one another in the same limitless way that God loves us.

ROMANS 8:1-11

Once Christ lives in us we shall be alive in four dimensions, as it were. He will give us the grace to embrace life with a fullness and generosity which is unfettered by self-interest or prejudice. And even death does not mark an end, but an entrance to the complete fullness of eternal life lived out for ever in the presence and kingdom of the risen Christ.

MARK 12:28-34

Regularly through Israel's history the prophets had declared God's loathing for lip worship without a committed heart, and hypocritical sacrifices that were empty of true repentance. Now, when the scribe approaches Jesus, he is genuinely concerned to find out where Jesus stands in relation to the Mosaic Law. Jesus focuses attention right back at the fundamental principles, from which all else springs, and the scribe warmly responds. He recognises that Christ is not a threat to the Law but is anxious to centralise what is really important, instead of looking so closely at the intricate rules and regulations that the basic rock is disregarded.

The Christian Church is not automatically immune from a similar near-sightedness. We need to be constantly rigorous in gazing steadfastly at our loving God, so as to avoid getting side-tracked in all the little extras that can distort our true vision.

8th Sunday after Pentecost

The fruit of the Spirit. The kind of tree we are will always be shown by the kind of fruit we bear. If we are rooted in Christ, we shall find that our lives blossom and fruit richly.

YEAR 1

EZEKIEL 36:24-28

Following the fall of Jerusalem, the exiled people of Israel need encouragement and hope. Although they have brought their downfall on themselves by their lax and corrupt behaviour, God speaks through Ezekiel to remind them of his steadfast love, and his promise to save them. It will not be a patched up job, but a thorough remaking – a complete new heart transplant, so to speak – until they are enabled to think and love as God does.

GALATIANS 5:16-25

We are all prone to self-indulgence, and Paul suggests that the only way to steer clear of it is to be guided by the Spirit. But what exactly does that mean? The Ezekiel passage gives us a clue. In order to save his people from themselves, God knew he would have to give them a new heart; Christ's victory opened the way for this to happen. For the outpouring of the Spirit penetrates our personalities and turns us into a new 'species', with natural capacity for strong growth, good fruit and resistance to disease.

The good fruit described in this passage, then, is not stuck on to the outside of us, where it would surely decay before long; rather, it grows quite naturally, without exaggerated effort, provided we are first remade by God into fruiting varieties!

JOHN 15:16-END

Jesus never promises us a rose garden. He never pretends that life in his service will be without danger and hardship. Often, in fact, he takes care to warn his friends that they are quite likely to be abused, just as he is. Saint Theresa is said to have been feeling low after such treatment, and heard God explain that this was the way he treated all his friends. No wonder, then, she retorted, that he had so few!

Yet, in spite of hardship, the fruiting goes on, and we still see wonderful examples of fruitful Christian lives whose joy, patience and love spread light among many. And when the going is painful or lonely, and we begin to wonder if God is still there, he is suddenly beside us, with assurance and encouragement, and we realise he has been through everything with us, just as he promised.

YEAR 2

EZEKIEL 37:1-14

When hope finishes, it is as if a candle gutters and dies; as if a heart misses a beat and stops. Carcasses remain, and many people's lives are littered with carcasses: their hopes are dead, and fester to rank bitterness. What chance is there of bringing such people back to life?

Often their despair is treated with drugs which may affect the outward symptoms, but if the cause is deep-seated anger and bitterness, because hopes have been dashed, the despair and depression cannot be cured by drugs alone.

This prophecy points to the only lasting and complete wholeness: the Spirit of God can awaken new life in the deadest, most hardened, and seemingly hopeless situations. Nothing is too dead or beyond his life-giving breath.

We who know Christ must work tirelessly to open the floodgates for that life to pour in; wedge a foot of love in the door to keep it open in those who are in danger of closing it completely; and constantly clear away all that clutters and blocks his love in our own lives.

I CORINTHIANS 12:4-13
His love is outpoured on his followers in a wealth of diversity, an abundance of gifts and talents, which are all valuable in building up Christ's Church.

It is no good wasting our time and God's in hankering after a different gift. Nor can we decide in advance our first choices and recommend God to take our advice!

God is so much greater than we often arrogantly imagine, and he sees, with complete knowledge and insight, what the needs are, and how and by whom they can be met. In some ways this makes life a good deal lighter and happier, for we have no need to worry any more about what we can or cannot do; instead we have only to love and trust Jesus, the Lord, and he will bring out in us all kinds of gifts which are often unexpected and sometimes a complete surprise and joy. Having been made rich, we can spend our gifts as liberally and freely as God wants; then, together, we will be helping to reap God's harvest.

LUKE 6:27-38
Some of Christ's basic teaching has been gathered here so that we can get a clear view of what 'loving', in God's vocabulary, really entails. What we hear is beyond all boundaries of reason and inclination, and involves becoming 'fools for Christ's sake'.

Since the words are so familiar, it is all too easy to assume that we know it, in the sense that we understand and have assimilated such an attitude in our own relationships.

But what about when we are unjustly accused?
    – unfairly treated?
    – upholding ideals against dangerous opposition?
Yet the way that Christ teaches has no list of exceptions

or special cases where the loving can be waived for expediency; it is an all-inclusive response to honouring every sordid scrap of humanity as being God-made and valuable. It is relinquishing all the independence of self until our lack of defensiveness leaves us free to serve.

9th Sunday after Pentecost

Putting on the whole armour of God. On our own we are not powerful enough to fight against evil, but God's power of goodness is sufficient for any evil we may meet, and he promises to give us that power when we put ourselves into his care.

YEAR 1

JOSHUA 1:1-9

Joshua, faced with the immense and dangerous task of leading the people of Israel right into the occupied promised land, is given great encouragement: he will be neither on his own, nor fighting only in his own strength. God promises to be with him wherever he goes. The only way he can block himself off from God's presence and power is by turning away from his Law.

If we sometimes feel cut off from God's power, it is a good idea to check that we have not erected blockades of selfishness, greed or pride which are preventing his power from getting through to us. It could be that God has not turned away from us at all; it is only that we have turned away from him.

EPHESIANS 6:10-20

There is no doubt that the evil against which we fight is real, dangerous, and immensely powerful. (One of the best ways to invite evil is to pretend it doesn't exist.) Paul was acutely aware of our need to be constantly vigilant, and well armed against it. He recognised that it could otherwise take over. History shows us that he was right.

So what of the future? Are we ever secretly afraid that evil is stronger even than God's influence in our world? Does it sometimes seem that we are doomed to lose the battle against it?

Whether we tend to dismiss evil or fear it, God's answer is the same: his power of goodness and love is infinite, and therefore well able to win. It is available for us to use, and we do need to use it – the whole lot, not just bits of it, which leave bits of us unprotected.

JOHN 17:11B-19

It is a great privilege to be given this insight into Jesus at prayer. We can learn so much from the way he pours out his heart to his Father, voicing his fears and talking things through in perfect trust. His love and affection for the little group he has trained is protective and deeply caring but not in any way possessive. Of far more importance than their personal bodily safety is that they are kept true to God, consecrated and set apart to that end. For love is stronger than death; when we live in God (who is Love) we live a life that can never be destroyed.

YEAR 2

I SAMUEL 17:37-50

This splendid story speaks of deep, spiritual truth. We see the simple weapons of trust in God and desire to do his will, contrasted with the cumbersome, exaggerated armour of bullying power. We see God-given freedom enabling natural gifts to flourish for good; we see that putting our faith in anything other than God, however technically advanced, may well let us down. We see that goodness can face evil and win; that if God is with us, we need not be afraid.

2 CORINTHIANS 6:3-10

There are extraordinary paradoxes in the Christian life. So many Christians have recorded the odd and remarkable experience of finding wonderful assurance and peace at the lowest, weakest and most terrifying points in their lives; of sensing the great company of the faithful while in solitary confinement, or inexplicable peace before execution. The right words pour out (often to our own astonishment!) when we are called to witness to Christ in a difficult situation; and when we know full well we would normally be exploding, we are buoyed up with patience that can have only one source.

These are the daily miracles that happen to all people of prayer. They strengthen our faith as we see that praying really works, and they witness powerfully to others – especially those who know our weaknesses and limitations all too well. For it all points to Christ's power working in us; and when other people see how our faith allows us to accept disaster calmly (not with a stiff upper lip, necessarily), to remain forgiving in the face of attack, or to stay outgoing during long-term illness, they will be drawn to seek this power for themselves.

MARK 9:14-29

Jesus and three of his disciples had just come down from the mountain where they had seen their master transfigured – an experience which increased their faith in him as the Son of God. Yet back here, Jesus is reminded of what a long way most of his followers have to go before they come anywhere near a committed faith – it must have often been rather depressing for Jesus, working with unbelieving, perverse humanity! Rather like coaxing a bonfire from damp sticks with one match on a windy day.

Jesus explains that the prayer essential for combatting the evil of this disease is closely linked with faith. Jesus' prayer, just witnessed at the top of the mountain, had completely transfigured him as he was seen full of God's glory. That radiance now floods out to the boy and heals him.

10th Sunday after Pentecost

The mind of Christ. It is, perhaps, his amazing humility which touches us most. For although he understands all things, not only on earth but in the entire universe, and although he is fully in charge, he was prepared to live and die among created beings in order to save them. He, the Lord, serves his people.

YEAR 1

JOB 42:1-6

Having endured terrible anguish, Job had finally challenged God to account for his suffering, and God had replied by directing Job to look afresh at the wonder and powerful beauty of the created universe. In the face of such overwhelming majesty, Job begins to realise something of the greatness of God, the creator. He understands that fulfilment comes to a person not through material possessions for the short space of one person's life span, but through the eternal values of dependence on God who is wider even than time, and beyond our complete comprehension.

PHILIPPIANS 2 1-11

Paul urges us to aim for the sky – to model our behaviour on Christ Jesus. And what shines out in his life is that incredible humility which made him willing to obey and to expend everything at colossal cost in order to help and save those he loved.

So, too, we are encouraged by the strength of Christ's love in us, to be outgoing, caring, generous and willing to put up with hardship and suffering in order to help and save others.

Internal bickering among Christian groups usually results from looking too much at each other and too little at Christ. If friction raises its ugly head, it is usually better if we break off everything we are doing for a while, and all look together at Christ. Then, having been touched again by his humility, open-mindedness, love and obedience, we shall be enabled to put our bickering right and heal our rifts, even if we still do not agree about a particular issue.

JOHN 13:1-15

The washing of the disciples' feet shows how Christ's love turns upside down the worldly structures of rights and privileges. This love means relinquishing everything, even our self-images which we cherish, in the business of serving others solely for love. Impossible? Yes, utterly impossible unless, by dying with Christ, we also live with him. In the eucharist which he has supplied, knowing our weakness, we are able to become one with him and share his life of love.

YEAR 2

I SAMUEL 24:9-17 (OR 1-17)

This is a very graphic description of the noble young David refusing to take advantage of Saul in spite of everything he has suffered at Saul's hands. The fact that Saul was once anointed by God sets him apart, as far as David is concerned, and in not taking revenge, David is honouring God.

If we believe that all people are made in God's likeness then we, too, must honour God in each person, whether we like what they do or not.

GALATIANS 6:1-10

In Christ we have a remarkable example of humility. As we see in the temptations, he could have used dramatic power to impress people into following him as a star; he preferred to choose the way of love, which never boasts, flaunts itself or takes advantage of others.

So in this letter to the Galatians, Paul reminds his readers of Christ's way of behaving. Even criticism, perhaps the hardest thing to learn to give lovingly or accept humbly, is under Christ's law of love and consideration for others. Such excellent behaviour can only happen through Christ's Spirit, of course. If only we remembered to make use of this precious and essential power, we would find ourselves far more able to behave in a Christlike way.

LUKE 7:36-END

Simon the Pharisee is a respected and honourable man, dutiful and fully committed to leading a good life. We may wonder what prompted him to invite Jesus to a meal at his house. Perhaps this surprisingly wise teacher from Nazareth spoke words so profound that he wanted to know more of him; perhaps he was merely sounding out a man who people were beginning to claim as a prophet. His lack of courtesy suggests that he did not rank Jesus as anyone very important. Whatever his reasons, he is certainly taken aback when Jesus seems quite unembarrassed by the attentions of a woman of bad reputation. The incident makes him suspect that Jesus may be an imposter. Jesus' response, however, proves him to be a prophet whose vision is wider and more fundamentally satisfying and practical than any before him. Simon is led to the point where he can see the link between love and forgiveness. The Law went hand in hand with con- demnation; Jesus brings it to life with reconciliation.

11th Sunday after Pentecost

Serving community. Our belief in Jesus as the Son of God is bound to lead on to serving the world as he did. Through our loving and unflinching service we proclaim to the world the generous, caring nature of God.

YEAR 1

ISAIAH 42:1-7

God may be powerful, but he is never heavy-handed or domineering. With great gentleness he tends the tiny flame of life, never snuffing it out or dismissing it. With our God there is always hope, for we are precious to our creator, and he will never give up on us, however slow we are to learn his ways, and however often we make mistakes.

If we, aware of that love, treat others in the same responsive and encouraging way, then they will come to understand God's love for them, too. That is our mission: to be lights that guide people to the peace and joy of a close relationship with God.

II CORINTHIANS 4:1-10

Such a mission is a great privilege but also carries enormous responsibility. After all, if we directed someone the wrong way to the Post Office they would only be lost for a short time, and the consequences would not be traumatic. But if we direct people to a false image of God's truth, we may be preventing them from finding his lasting joy and peace, which is far more serious.

So it is very important that we treasure God's light that he has entrusted to us, and never get illusions that we are anything but earthenware pots to contain it. That way we shall be able to help spread the light of Christ into the world's darkness.

JOHN 13:31-35

The best encouragement of all is that Jesus has been glorified by the Father, and in him we can begin to understand how love transforms and fulfils humanity. But we do not have to gaze longingly from a distance and struggle ineptly on our own: the very love which suffuses Jesus makes him reach out personally to us and help us.

YEAR 2

I CHRONICLES 29:1-9

Years before, David had wanted to build a house for his Lord, and the time had not been right. Now, with God's blessing, the work is about to begin under the care of Solomon, David's son. Notice how David had never abandoned the idea, but had patiently waited on the Lord's time, preparing through those years materials that would be useful when the building started. It is David's enthusiasm and dedication to serve God in this way that inspires all the generous gifts of gold, silver, bronze and iron which immediately come pouring in.

PHILIPPIANS 1:1-11

There is obviously a strong bond of affection between Paul and the Christians at Philippi. He draws a great deal of encouragement from the knowledge that they are working with him for the spread of the Gospel. Any work is less daunting and more fun when you know others are doing their bit as well. Surely that is partly why Christ founded the Church; working together for the kingdom, we can encourage one another along the way, sympathise, inspire and support. In the process we shall be changing increasingly into reflectors of Jesus.

MATTHEW 20:1-16

Humans are often blinkered when it comes to justice. Generosity in justice rouses suspicions that we may be losing out, and that would never do. Being competitive, we usually feel rather grudging when we meet people who are good at everything and even look attractive as well; we also spend time squashing these feelings in favour of good sportsmanship, but their existence cannot be denied.

In God's kind of justice there is joy for everyone who turns to him, especially those who looked as if they were heading for destruction but finally received God into their hearts, or those who have had such little help and guidance and yet turn to Christ.

If we are really living in Christ ourselves, we shall start to share his generous-hearted way of looking at things, rejoicing in people's gifts and the good use they are making of them, and delighting in newcomers to the Church bringing freshness and different outlooks to enrich and enliven the worship.

12th Sunday after Pentecost

The Church as a witnessing community. Since we are the members of Christ's body, it is our witness and example that will either repel or draw others to seek God's face. Unless we display Christ's love, many will never see it.

YEAR 1

ISAIAH 49:1-6

God is a personal God – he works through individuals. When a whole nation is chosen to witness to him, it is possible for their light to spread far and wide. Beginning with internal commitment, repentance and reconciliation among the chosen people, God goes on to a far bigger plan, much more far-reaching than the prophet had envisaged; in time every nation will be able to participate in God's work of salvation.

God's power is enormous, and he will use us, if we co-operate, to take on even the deadliest evils of our time and defeat them. When we fail to co-operate, we are limiting his power in our lives and our world; we do so at our peril.

2 CORINTHIANS 5:14-6:2

Whenever we catch glimpses of God's astounding glory, we are overwhelmed by the sense of our own unworthiness for the patient and loving way he deals with us. For, as Paul points out, if we were to get what we deserve for our sins, we should all be dead! But because the great, creating God was willing to die in our place, it is our sin and selfishness which dies with him, enabling us to live on in a new creation, provided we bind ourselves to Christ.

It is a constant 'dying', whenever sin sidles or charges into our relationships and behaviour; but it is also a constant 'resurrection' as we are tenderly shaped and moulded into new creatures filled with the life of our risen Lord.

JOHN 17:20-END

The kind of unity Jesus prays for in his followers is the same loving relationship he has with and in his Father. They are of the same mind and the same spirit. It is a wonderful vision for us to keep before us as we struggle to mend rifts that have cut deep through history, or stand at the edge of new rifts which threaten to yawn open and divide God's people. God himself is the only power which can bind us in loving unity, even when we disagree about certain issues.

The way we discuss or argue should witness to the way of thinking which results from living in Christ.

Year 2

MICAH 4:1-5

Although the ancient prophecies were fulfilled in Jesus, that is not where they end. We always have to remember that we are in the final stage of God's salvation, accomplished through Christ who was the first fruit of the harvest of life. Still to come is the complete accomplishment of God's will; the total establishment of his kingdom which is now growing in the hearts of many in each generation.

Micah's prophecy includes this Day of the Lord which will come at the end of time, brought about by the millions of burning lights of witnesses to the one true light. It is our privilege to be among those light-bearers.

ACTS 17:22-END

There were altars to all kinds of deities in Athens. The altar to the unknown god was a sort of spiritual insurance policy, in case someone got angry at being left out. Paul takes advantage of such an opening to tell them all about God. He explains him in terms of their own experience – that he is the creator, from whom spring all the things they have endowed with holiness. He acknowledges their religions but draws on a stage further, to acknowledge the power behind all life. So far, so good.

It is when he starts talking about the raising of the dead – something impossible – that many scoff and go their way. For this is the mind-stretching thing about our religion: the same God who powerfully created the universe also involved himself personally in our world. Once we accept that Jesus is the Son of God, his resurrection is in keeping with what we know of God's power. But the only way to account for God becoming man is to recognise in the incarnation an unimaginably powerful capacity for love.

MATTHEW 5:13-16

We, who have been entrusted with the building up of God's kingdom on earth, must, without fail, recognise the source of our power and pass the glory on to God. Otherwise we are not working for him, but for ourselves, and that is both dangerous and destructive.

Salt was not just a seasoning but a food preserver, so that it was actually important for life. Worldly, material values have a powerful grip on many people's minds. The greed and selfishness they engender can cause decay and rot in family life, society, and in individuals. We, the Church, are the salt which can preserve, purify and decontaminate: that is how vital our work as Christ's body is. It is desperately important for our world that we are effective grains of salt.

Similarly with light: we may all be burning brightly with God's love due to our worship and communion with our heavenly Father, but if we share his love only with other Christians we shall be hiding our light under a tub. We Christians are supposed to be the world's light: is its darkness due to our wasted, under-used or dim light? If we do not shine, how will anyone see?

13th Sunday after Pentecost

Just as Christ suffered, so we also will suffer. But the suffering is not negative and demoralising; it is even cause for rejoicing, because through the crucifixion and death of Christ came the resurrection. As we share his suffering we shall also share his glorious life.

YEAR 1

ISAIAH 50:4-9A

The physical and psychological cruelty endured without retaliation here, foresees the mocked and crucified Christ, in heart-rending clarity. We sense the terrible rejection, the jeering and lack of understanding; but there is also the help and strength from God which empowers the suffering servant to submit to his agony in the knowledge that it is necessary for a greater good.

Suffering in our own lives can provide really fertile conditions for growth, much as we may laugh at the stupidity of such an idea in our initial anger, distress and hopelessness. The value of suffering is partly in the way it can nudge us into trusting God instead of our own strength which is in short supply. It helps us learn what it means to be dependent on God and draw help from him. It heightens our awareness of the suffering of others and will in the future enable us to be more sympathetic and useful. It gives us a glimpse of the suffering that Christ was willing to undergo, in order to buy us back from sin; and it can concentrate our attention on what is of lasting value, rather than living from one distraction to the next.

Suffering is bound to be acutely painful; but with Christ it can become a positive pain.

ACTS 7:54-8:1

Stephen was so convinced of Jesus' eternal presence that death was a gateway to a life more rich and fulfilling than anything this world could offer. Sometimes we confess this belief with our words, but the way we behave denies it. Are we really convinced that God will keep his promises, even when a loved one is at the point of death, or when witnessing to Christ threatens our popularity or our lifestyle?

Being children of eternity does not preclude grief and heartache: in the person of Jesus we see that love is often compatible with tears. Yet it does mean that at bedrock level when we are confronted with the bleak, barren landscape of despair, Jesus alone, Lord of earth and heaven, time and eternity, reaches across death, across annihilation, and keeps his word to be one with us for ever, in this world and the world to come.

JOHN 16:1-11

Knowing this gives us hope and courage, even in the face of Jesus' warnings here. Anyone who loves becomes vulnerable, so if we are set on course to love in God's way, we are bound to get involved with suffering, even apart from such dangers as persecution. But Jesus does not only warn, he also provides. The Helper, or Comforter, will give us whatever we need to cope, survive and rejoice.

YEAR 2

JEREMIAH 20:7-11A

Things were not going too well for Jeremiah. He was ridiculed, belittled and abused; the message of gloom and doom did not go down well, however true it was, and he was very tempted to give up the whole business, keep quiet and let people get on with their destruction unchecked.

The trouble was, he knew that God needed him to speak out, and since he loved God, that placed him in a tricky and painful dilemma. His love for God won and he was then prepared to put up with any insults and ill-treatment for the sake of following the God he worshipped.

If we find ourselves in the minority, with values that are despised and scorned by many around us, and pressures on our children to conform to different standards of behaviour, we may well feel like Jeremiah. It will test our reasons for standing out; if we have been working towards gaining adulation and respect, then these difficulties will probably dissuade us and cause us to falter. If, on the other hand, we are giving our lives for our love of God, then we shall find that the difficulties deepen our resolve and give us clearer understanding of how important the work is.

ACTS 20:17-35

Paul is no stranger to suffering, either. He lives a very insecure life, by most standards, and insists on sticking his neck out to say and do what he believes is God's will, even when it results in hardship and risk. So why does he bother?

Paul lives both in time and in eternity since receiving the ever-living Spirit; so physical safety and a long life no longer hold the same importance for him. It is spiritual life that lasts for ever which is more important, and he is quite happy to do anything to help others believe it.

For Paul knows that when you do, it gives you freedom and peace and joy that you wouldn't have thought possible.

MATTHEW 10:16-22

So we do not have to fear any more. If Christ wants us to witness with words we can be sure he will give us the right, suitable words to say. He will give us an uncanny sense of calm as we stand up for what is right or speak out against what is wrong, even if some ridicule us for it.

That is because it is not us speaking at all; it is none other than the holy Spirit of God.

14th Sunday after Pentecost

The family. God loves and cares for us, his children, with parental love, and we are a spiritual family, with Christ our brother. Our own relationships should reflect this strong bond of love and affection; the kind of love which is not possessive but liberating.

YEAR 1

PROVERBS 31:10-END

In spite of the fact that few wives work assiduously at their distaffs these days, there is something in this account of the perfect wife which has a lot to say to all modern members of God's family.

It is the thoughtful care for others, shown in work; or, as Kahlil Gibran puts it, 'work is love made visible'. A carefully prepared meal, a well-ironed shirt or a newly decorated room – whoever does these things and whoever they are done for, they tell a great deal about love.

There is little value in love being expressed in words if no demonstration of practical caring is ever forthcoming. Christianity is a 'body' religion; after all, our God wore a body in order to show his love for us. And, using our bodies to work, carefully and lovingly, we are making our lives a prayer of praise.

EPHESIANS 5:25-6:4

Paul uses marriage as a beautiful illustration of the kind of relationship Christ has with his Church. At first sight it may look as if Paul's concept of marriage is irrelevant in our age of sexual equality, and is one of those bits of the Bible we can skip lightly over, looking the other way.

Look again. Obedience sometimes gets stuck in the groove of grudging duty, and love in the groove of emotion and instinctive desire; but what happens when Love becomes Law, as it has in Christ? Now, duty and obedience become full of delight and joy, freely chosen and always appreciated. This can only occur when both husband and wife live in obedience to the Law of Love, with all the patience, acceptance, kindness and humility that it entails.

And that is the sort of marriage Christ has with his Church: bound by love, the Church becomes one with the body of Christ; our obedience to him springs out of our love for him and his rich love for us.

MARK 10:2-16

It is clear from Jesus' teaching here that God's will concerning marriage is that it should be between one woman and one man and that it should be a life-long partnership. Just as Jesus had developed the Mosaic law, about loving your neighbour, to include loving your enemy, so he develops the Mosaic rule concerning divorce. Under the new covenant, based on unlimited, selfless love, we are called to be so responsive to God and each other that our marriages work for life.

Unfortunately, it is very obvious that 'hardness of heart' still tears marriages apart, resulting in misery and heartbreak for parents and children alike. The break-up of strong family units is damaging the whole structure of our society; and there are many pressures to accept marriage as only a temporary state, valid until it becomes tiresome or inconvenient.

As with all Jesus' teaching about real loving, we are being asked the impossible. It only becomes possible when our whole life is founded not on our partner, our emotions, our instincts or society's expectations, but on the rock of Christ. He can reinforce crumbling marriages, heal deep hurts, refresh our love, promote forgiveness and soften hardened attitudes, so he is an excellent guest to invite to the wedding!

But we also need to remember that our God is loving and compassionate, understanding our weakness and willing to forgive. So if we have a wrecked or failed marriage in our past, we are not unredeemable; when we confess our failure and determine to build our future on Christ, he will not only forgive us but also give back the years that the locusts have eaten.

YEAR 2

GENESIS 45:1-15

This is a very moving account of a family reunion and reconciliation. Joseph is so overwhelmed with love for his brothers that he has completely forgiven them for all their mistreatment of him so many years before. His concern now is to care for them in the future, and he dismisses their former cruelty in a way which makes it clear that no resentment or bitterness has been harboured through the intervening years.

If there are any estrangements in our family, perhaps this passage can give us the courage to set about reconciliation. Perhaps, as here, the first move must come from the wronged, rather than the offender.

EPHESIANS 3:14-END

All necessary courage, determination, humility and strength will be supplied for any act of love or reconciliation we decide on when Christ lives in us. For the great Father of us all is like a loving parent of a huge, sprawling family; the archetypal parent who embodies selfless love, creation and nurture. The glory we give him witnesses to the unlimited power he is able to set working in our lives.

LUKE 11:1-13

The disciples could see that when Jesus prayed it was an altogether different experience from the praying they knew.

What he taught was not so much a form of words as a new relationship with God. Just as we would expect our children to be given good things from their earthly father, so we, as God's children, can trustingly ask and expect to receive good things from our heavenly Father.

It is sometimes helpful to think of the Lord's Prayer as headings, and spend much longer on each phrase than is usual, remembering, throughout each phrase and silence, that God is our loving Father and we are conversing with him as his loving children.

15th Sunday after Pentecost

Those in authority. All authority stems from God, and when temporal leaders remember this, good government results. Corruption in authority begins when God's supremacy is ignored, rejected or usurped. For us, as citizens of heaven through God's grace, loyalty to God's kingdom must always come first; that may well be shown by our loyalty to others in authority.

YEAR 1

ISAIAH 45:1-7

The powerful Cyrus was about to break Babylon's rule; perhaps this would be the way in which the people of Israel could be freed from Babylonian captivity. It seemed to the prophet that Cyrus would actually be used for God's will to be accomplished.

It is certainly true that God works through many and varied means, using a far wider spectrum than those who know him. They may not believe in him, but he believes in them; and if many of us pray fervently for all those who lead and have influence in national and international affairs, God's plans will be put into practice in the most unexpected ways and through surprising people.

For God is more powerful than any individual or group, no matter how important or aggressive it may temporarily seem. Even in the worst horrors of war and disease, some shaft of hope and goodness lights up among the terrible shadows; even evils can be used by the one creative and caring God to bring about the birth of hope and understanding. This is because our God reigns – over all time, in all places and throughout all existence, whether excellent or appalling.

ROMANS 13:1-7

When any state upholds justice and order, respect for people and property and maintenance of personal safety, it will be acting under God, whether using his name or not. And we are to respect and keep within its laws, not just for the sake of steering clear of punishment, but because our consciences guide us to do so.

Obviously Paul is not advocating blind obedience even when a corrupt state demands action which is contrary to Christian teaching. At such times we need to be among those who stand up for what is right. But as far as possible we are advised to show that as followers of Christ we can obey cheerfully, respect others' positions and values, and be responsible citizens.

MATTHEW 22:15-22

The Pharisees have been faced directly with the need to turn their expectations and thinking upside down if they are to be saved. But they have, like Dives, the wealthy man, too much to lose, and so begin scheming for the downfall of this man who threatens their comfortable lives.

Cleverly, they lay the trap for Jesus to fall into: Roman taxes are a volcanic issue and if he denounces them the authorities will be enraged; but if he does not, his integrity as a Jewish teacher will be in question. The scheming is particularly ironic, since it hinges on the forfeiting of esteem – the very thing the Pharisees themselves could not cope with.

So Jesus not only confounds them, but also uses the situation to teach, if they will only listen. The real question is one of priorities, and whereas what Caesar both represents and requires is money, or materialism, what we owe God is on a different plane altogether – more costly, more demanding, more far-reaching, but also more fulfilling and rewarding.

YEAR 2

I KINGS 3:4-15

Solomon's legendary choice of gift, and God's pleasure at it, has been echoed in stories of similar nobility in many other cultures. It does, after all, show man at his possible best, rather than in his more usual human petty-mindedness. We may hope we would choose a similarly noble gift, but have a sneaking suspicion that, on the spur of the moment, we might well have plumped for a repaired car (to make us more useful, of course) or a bigger house (so as to be more hospitable).

Solomon was feeling rather vulnerable. He was conscious of his raw youth, aware of his inexperience and probably very nervous about the daunting prospect of ruling the people of Israel. In some ways all that put him at a disadvantage; yet in another, important way, his misgiving gave him an advantage, because whenever we are at our most vulnerable, and most aware of our weakness, we are also at our most receptive. There is no play-acting about trusting in prayer, when people are confronted with the possibility of immediate death in an accident or disaster. Desperate people are driven to pray, and there are many stories of fervent prayer during shipwrecks. or while waiting for rescue.

In Solomon's vulnerability he asks for what he needs, instead of what he wants. It is something we need to cultivate in our prayers, so that, instead of thinking of short term answers we would like to suggest God tries, we acknowledge the actual difficulties of our own weaknesses, and leave it in his hands. Things are far more likely to fall into place if we do.

I TIMOTHY 2:1-7
We are encouraged to pray for all those in authority; not merely as a dutiful lip-service but with the deeply concerned Christian love which supports and is prepared to act and become involved.

There are two reasons for this prayer. One is that, obviously, good government allows us to live peaceful lives, free from terror and violence.

The second reason is that, whether we agree with our leaders or not, whether they are Christian or not, whether they are interested in us or not, they are in God's eyes loved beings whom he has created. God longs for everyone to be saved – that, after all, is why he bothered with the humiliating business of becoming man!

If we live in Christ, we shall start to see everyone through his eyes, and that will urge us to pray.

MATTHEW 14:1-12

Herod's obsessive guilt is typical of the misery which results from using authority for corrupt and cruel acts. Herod had known that what he did was evil; yet he had been too weak to follow his conscience, and instead had given in to the request of his jealous and bitter wife.

For us, too, there are times when we may have to refuse to follow the law because it would be against God's law. If this happens, we can be sure that, however much hardship, exile or danger it brings us, we shall be eternally safe, buoyed up by the encouraging presence of God.

16th Sunday after Pentecost

Loving our neighbour. Since God made all of us – even those we may not like or whose behaviour we may disapprove of – we are to love one another and help those in need, regardless of whether they are friends of ours or not.

YEAR 1

LEVITICUS 19:9-18

The message which Moses is given for the children of Israel concerns God's call for them to be holy. Holiness will be expressed by love, and love will be expressed by forgiveness.

Such a message is reassuring, for although the ideal of holiness is distressingly impossible, the path towards it does not presuppose perfect beings who never irritate each other or offend. Since we know we all spend considerable time (and even effort!) in irritating and offending each other, it is good news to find there is hope for us yet.

For the holy loving to which we are called is about how we react to our own sin and that of other people. It is about forgiving, in the sense of really wiping the offence away; if we dredge it up years later in a spiteful argument we have not really forgiven at all. Nor must we tot up the injustices we have suffered and store them ready for some mammoth explosion of rage and 'righteous' indignation. Far better to talk about what has upset us, being ready to hear the other point of view, recognising that, unlikely as it may seem, we may actually be mistaken or be over-reacting. Then, with full forgiveness, our loving will have developed, and we shall have progressed along the road to holiness.

ROMANS 12:9-END

This passage is one we could usefully fix up on the kitchen, office or factory wall, or even learn off by heart. There is really practical advice here for living under God's authority in a positive and inspiring way. The whole idea is really summed up in those last words: 'Do not be overcome with evil, but overcome evil with good,'

As Christians we need to do positive good rather than being simply mild, inoffensive people. God's power can give us authority and confidence to inspire others by our behaviour.

LUKE 10:25-37

This Gospel shows us how, all too easily, our mouths can utter honourable vows of commitment which our lives belie. We can probably think of many vows we have made which we thought, at the time, we understood, but only later discovered what was really entailed. Perhaps we may regret ever having promised anything, at that point!

But if we have kept the vow even in the hard times, we can look back gratefully to the way the difficulties have enabled us to grow. The lawyer who approaches Jesus thinks that he understands the Law inside out and back to front. He is really hoping to make a fool of this new upstart.

Jesus shows him, in the story of the Good Samaritan, what the Law really entails when it has soaked into a person's whole being. It is no longer a case of doing certain things and not doing certain other things. It involves the much more open-ended and therefore far costlier commitment which sees with eyes of love, recognises needs with insight, and works for another's good without counting the cost.

YEAR 2

DEUTERONOMY 15:7-11

Even the best rules tend to get frayed at the edges after a time, and need tightening up again. This seven year rule, whereby every debt is cancelled, and slaves can go free, is an efficient way of checking that no one is left destitute. Unfortunately, some of the people are keeping an eye out for the approach of the seventh year, and are noticeably less willing to lend to their poorer relatives as the time draws near for all debts to be cancelled. Rules only work when the generous spirit of them is adhered to.

I JOHN 4:15-END

We are so used to seeing the power of hatred in action. Terrorism, violent crimes, child abuse, revenge killings – the news is packed with details of destructive behaviour by individuals and nations based on hatred and fear.

At first sight it does look powerful. Innocent people lie dying as the murderer escapes with both life and money; aggressive threats extract secrets; brutal selfishness can pile up easy money quickly.

Yet through the history of the chosen people of Israel, and in the person of Jesus, God unfolds a much stronger power, which not only makes living more joyful and secure, but actually works better as well. Loving our enemies annihilates them more effectively than any gun can, because the door is then opened towards friendship. Rebels can be won over by kindness and a genuine concern for their cause, while repression and strong-arm tactics are more likely to turn them into underground revolutionaries. Love has inspired people to great acts of loyalty and courage and prolonged self-sacrifice; love has succeeded in uniting families and countries when war has weakened both and failed to bring lasting peace.

God's way of living by love, through every situation without exception, is both profound wisdom and sound good sense.

LUKE 16:19-END

People often express the view that they do not need to go to church because they are happy as they are and don't do anyone any harm. Dives, the rich man, didn't do anyone any harm. His sin was that he didn't do anyone any good either. Opportunities for helping and caring simply went past unnoticed: he did not realise they existed until it was too late. How can we be sure that we are not also missing opportunities to do good? It is very difficult to look at ourselves objectively but we need to train ourselves to do it regularly if we want to find out in time.

The more closely we live to Jesus, the more enlightened we shall become about where the needs are and how we can help. For we have not only Moses and the prophets to guide us, but also Jesus, risen and glorified, so we cannot say we have not been told. The ball is in our court.

17th Sunday after Pentecost

The kind of life we lead proclaims the kind of faith we have. We may say we believe in God, but that is only true if we live a life compatible with belief in the God of love. It will be our kindness, thoughtfulness, self-control and generosity which best prove our faith real.

YEAR 1

JEREMIAH 7:1-11

Hypocrisy can so easily slip into our religion without our noticing, and we all have to guard against it constantly. As humans we tend to be lazy, and as soon as we get slack about our self-discipline in prayer and worship, we can find ourselves starting to behave the way 'everybody else does', while still singing our praises lustily each Sunday.

The people of Israel were just the same, and had begun to adopt the ways of the heathen cultures around them, probably without noticing. Jeremiah's words remind them and us that God will not tolerate double standards. If we are going to proclaim faith in him we must ditch all behaviour and attitudes that are contrary to his values of love, respect for one another, and purity of heart.

JAMES 1:16-END

The practical James knows that the Word must always be a spring-board to action, and not a substitute for it. It is quite possible to be swept up on to an emotional 'high' during some inspiring worship, and feel so good about it that we fail to notice glaring needs and opportunities for serving when we get out of the church. Or we can get so used to talking 'God-language' that we deceive ourselves into thinking we are practising the words we spout, when we have actually got stuck in a complacent rut.

Another temptation is to busy about all the doing, without any hearing first. (Or during; or afterwards) God's word is our treasure, our strength and our foundation, and if we really steep ourselves in it, by attentive reading and receptive contemplation, we shall find ourselves urged to take positive action in ways which may surprise us. So long as we do not let Self plug up the channels, God's Word will flow through us for the good of the world.

LUKE 17:11-19

The lepers must have had faith in Jesus. They all asked him to take pity on them, and did not hesitate to set off to show themselves to the priest as cleansed men while their bodies were still covered with sores.

It is a mark of Jesus' immense love for us that he never sets our thanks and adoration as a condition of helping us, even though he longs for it. He loves us enough to leave us free to make our own decisions and never forces us to honour him.

Yet how mean and small-minded, how arrogant and discourteous we are if we fail to give God the thanks and credit he deserves, when we have cried to him in distress and he has taken pity on us and healed us.

People pray when they are suddenly aware of their frailty and vulnerability. If we stay with him right through to thankfulness we shall be doubly blessed and the Kingdom of God will be that much closer.

YEAR 2

JEREMIAH 32:6-15

Jeremiah is in prison; Jerusalem is under seige; all immediate hope for the people of Israel living freely in their own land is quite dead. And yet, at this lowest point, Jeremiah proclaims his faith in the future of God's people by putting his money where his faith is: he buys a plot of land at his village of

Anathoth from his cousin. Since there is no chance of using it yet, the deeds are preserved in an earthenware jar, ready for the time Jeremiah is convinced will come, when the land will once again belong to God's people. It is a remarkable act of trust in God.

GALATIANS 2:15-3:9

Paul had been a very committed and conscientious rabbi, following the Law astutely. He is therefore well qualified to speak on this question bothering the Galatians: the importance of the Law in being saved and liberated from one's sins. If anyone could find salvation by strict adherence to God's Mosaic Law, it would be Paul himself.

Yet he confidently asserts that the Law, though valuable as a guideline, creates its own type of prison for although it suggests a good, noble and godly way of living, it does not provide the strength and power which weak humanity desperately needs in order to achieve such a life.

With the coming of Jesus Christ, all this changed. God, humbling himself in becoming man, accepts the duties and confines of the Law, but also breaks through them to suffuse them with his own life and power. So, when we accept Christ, we too are enabled to plug into that power which can at last take us just as we are, without pretence, and make us new creatures, able to do all things; for it is no longer us, but Christ alive and working in us and through us.

18th Sunday after Pentecost

Offering our lives to God's service. God has given us so much that our thankfulness prompts us to show our love in acts of generosity, both to God in worship, and to one another wherever there is need.

YEAR 1

DEUTERONOMY 26:1-11

The people are reminded here that, during their hardship and suffering in Egypt, God heard them and acted powerfully to rescue them. It is both a duty and a pleasure then, for them to acknowledge this by an annual thanksgiving and harvest offering. Thankfulness and gratitude find expression in practical ways, and generosity often awakes generosity in the recipient.

II CORINTHIANS 8:1-9

Here again, suffering that the Church in Macedonia has undergone seems to have made them extra generous to others in need. Suffering can have this power of making us more aware of others' needs and more sympathetic. Their giving, we notice, does not stem from a desire to look good, but from their offering of themselves to God. He translates that offering into cheerful, loving service to others.

MATTHEW 5:17-26

Jesus was not punctilious about observing the exact letter of the Law. On a number of occasions he healed on the Sabbath instead of resting from all work, and this raised doubts and righteous anger in others.

So Jesus takes pains to explain the purpose of God's Law. He shows the people not only its limitations but also its demands. Instead of conserving narrow, pedantic behaviour, the Law is now thrown open so that in one sense we are freed from exclusive and rigid rules and in others we are given the grown-up responsibility of observing God's loving will in all its awesome ideals.

Our whole selves are to be brought under his Law in this way – what we think as well as how we act; what is hidden as well as what is seen by others.

Since rules define limits, the temptation is to go no further than they explicitly demand. That gives us a sense of having 'done our duty' and 'arrived'. When Jesus speaks of the Law as complete loving, the limits are swept away, and we can see that there is no point at which we will have completed our duty, for the duty of love in God's terms has no boundary.

YEAR 2

NEHEMIAH 6:1-16 OR ECCLESIASTICUS 38:24-END

Both these passages praise the perseverance that is shown in working long hours, often in the face of difficulties, in order to complete a valuable piece of work. Their patience and concentration becomes in some way an act of prayer and praise to God whom they serve.

With us, too, our work can be part of our praise and worship; we should not cut that area off as being 'secular'; with God, all the different parts of our life can be used, and all are an extension of our life in him.

I PETER 4:7-11

Although Peter's advice springs out of the expectation that the end of the world was imminent, it is still good advice which will remind us we are only travellers through this life, and not dwellers in it. We are not owners but stewards, so it is only right that we pass on any gifts we have received in service to others.

MATTHEW 25:14-30

Some people keep their best china permanently behind glass doors; some have precious jewellery in bank vaults instead of round their necks; some keep a large 'nest-egg' of money and rarely dip into it, even if the carpet is threadbare.

All these precautions are taken because greatly valued things are precious, and we want to preserve them from damage. But the need to preserve can get out of hand, until, since we are not using something, we come to value its value, rather than itself. And then, in a way, its possible use is being wasted.

Gifts and talents are often under-used and hidden away as well. Sometimes this is because of an inverted vanity, rather than real modesty; perhaps other people will not appreciate our gift sufficiently – they may even laugh at our efforts.

Sometimes we hold back because our sophisticated society brings a slick professionalism into every home through the media, and homegrown talent is thought of as second best.

What Jesus wants us to know is that we are all valuable and have all been given talents which can be used to good effect in our world. We really ought to use them, or the world will suffer – yes, even if one, seemingly meagre talent is wasted, the world will be poorer.

If we are willing to have a go, try anything once, or make fools of ourselves in a good cause, we might well unearth talents we did not even know we had!

19th Sunday after Pentecost

Living by faith. Faith is what gives us hope and certainty about things we can't actually see. It enables us to step out confidently into the future, and it gives us courage in the face of threats and danger.

YEAR 1

GENESIS 28:10-END

God chooses the strangest people to be his close friends! The character we have been shown in Jacob up to this point in his life hardly suggests a man of goodness, honesty or responsibility. But God could see the man he would make him into, and chooses him to be the next link in the chain of Promise.

Having cheated his brother Esau out of their father's blessing, Jacob is on the run. And here God makes himself powerfully known, confirming the blessing and making it clear that, faults or not, God has chosen Jacob. The effect on the guilty, scheming Jacob is utter amazement, reverence and the beginning of a new, deep faith; from now on he is going to trust God .

HEBREWS 11:1-2, 8-16

Faith, or trust in God, is the firm ground on which we stand as we journey towards a deeper relationship with our Creator. It is unaffected by our moods, feelings, state of health or the weather. It is not altered by hardship, suffering, success or failure.

How can anything so constant exist in us who, being human, are generally inconstant? The reason is that it is nothing man-made or man-invented. It is a present which God will give us if we ask him for it. His close friends, from Abraham onwards, have known it and lived in its hope, and that is why it is so strong – it is based on a hope which is certain and goes deeper and further even than death.

MATTHEW 6:24-END

In fact, we are easily put off by outside influences. So many trivial things seem important, and we are not helped by the vast amount of advertising, which aims to create a need and then fill it. An offshoot of this is that many cravings and expectancies are roused which give rise to guilt and anxiety when they cannot be fulfilled.

Many of us waste time and energy worrying about what shape we are; which clothes we should wear; whether our children are intelligent, brave, relaxed, fat, thin, noisy or quiet enough; whatever would happen if. . . and so on.

Life is not only more pleasant, but a good deal healthier if we take this teaching of Jesus to heart. It only demands a change of attitude, not necessarily life-style. If we begin every day by consciously submitting our energy and resources to working with God, and putting our worries into his capable hands, the pressure is immediately eased. Praying people have been found to acquire the therapeutic alpha brain waves, so praying is good for you in many ways!

Worrying is also connected with pride and selfishness. We may feel very self-righteous about worrying for those we love, thinking that it proves our love. But isn't it sometimes an inflated sense of our own importance which makes us worry, assuming that we have the key to other people's happiness and survival? If we acknowledge that the key really belongs to God, then we can start seeing that the world will not crumble if we forget the peas, or our children do not make the grades we hoped for, or we have to get used to new neighbours.

With God at the helm, problems can become exciting opportunities, and we shall be able to face whatever life throws in our way with confidence and enthusiasm.

YEAR 2

DANIEL 6:10-23

The Bible is full of inspiring stories, and this must be one of the best loved. Daniel's quiet trust in God pulses through it like the rhythm of his daily prayers, unswerving even in the face of danger. He has obviously influenced King Darius for good already, and Darius is clearly very fond of his friend, who has such faith in his God. We feel for him as he works till sunset to negotiate Daniel's case for freedom from the rules but in the end he submits to pressure and agrees to treat Daniel like everyone else. We can imagine him pacing the palace floor through the night, fasting and perhaps praying to Daniel's God.

So it is the faith of two fine people which protects Daniel. It results in relief and delight as Daniel's familiar voice pipes up from the lions' den and there is great rejoicing all round.

ROMANS 5:1-11

Paul reminds us that we are not in a state of grace through our own efforts but through the person of Jesus, so we must always guide people's praise for any good we may do towards Christ, in whose strength we live and work. Even suffering provides opportunities to boast of God's love, for out of suffering can spring patience, perseverance and hope: the strong hope which comes from trusting in the all powerful, loving God.

LUKE 19:1-10

Zacchaeus must have presented rather a comic picture to the citizens of Jericho, standing on tiptoe to peer over the crowd and then climbing a sycamore tree, in spite of his wealth and status. Why was he so curious? Perhaps he was a lonely man, for all his riches. Perhaps he already felt vaguely uneasy about his life-style, but hadn't the courage to change without some firm outside incentive.

Whatever his reasons, Jesus' heart goes out to him when he sees him. He senses Zacchaeus' need to be useful and valuable, his longing to be wanted. So he gives him a practical job to do, and then there is no stopping Zacchaeus who cannot wait to get started.

Jesus' outgoing friendship gives him the impetus to respond to others and put right the wrongs Zacchaeus has done. We can almost see the chains of misery dropping off him as he begins his new life of freedom through love. As Christ's ambassadors, we can set other Zacchaeuses free.

20th Sunday after Pentecost

Steadfast endurance. By his own example and encouragement, Jesus inspires us to continue faithful even through the difficult and rough passages of life; in fact, it is often through such perseverance that we are enabled to mature spiritually, and grow to fulfill our potential.

YEAR 1

DANIEL 3:13-26

Shadrach, Meshach and Abednego are faced with death if they refuse to worship Nebuchadnezzar's god or the idol he has set up. Their determination to stay true to God's command is put to the test, and their steadfast faith is remarkable; they refuse to worship the idol even if their God does not rescue them!

Such endurance under pressure provided just the kind of role pattern needed by the people of Israel, who were exiled and living among pagan worshippers. Such examples would have inspired them, in their own endurance tests, to stay loyal and true to God through everything.

ROMANS 8:18-25

Paul's life was full of hardship, danger and deprivation as he spent it in spreading the Good News of Jesus. The patient hope which he describes is not a grim determined stoicism but a joyful acceptance of being part of a larger plan than immediate problems; a plan which is totally in the hands of the loving God he trusts with his life.

LUKE 9:51-END

In this reading we see both Jesus' and man's commitment. Firstly, Jesus, fully aware of the distress and agony he is certain to encounter, nevertheless resolutely takes the road to

Jerusalem, obedient to his calling, regardless of the risks and costs.

Secondly, we see several examples of men offering to follow or being called. 'I will follow you wherever you go,' says one. We sense in Jesus' reply that perhaps the man was not fully aware of the hardships and discomforts his decision would entail.

Others make excuses for not immediately obeying their call. Their reasons may seem humane and valid, but this is not really the point. They serve to point out how radical and absolute our approach to Christ must be: we are little use to him unless we are prepared to commit ourselves wholeheartedly.

YEAR 2

GENESIS 32: 22-30

Having had the reassurance of God's blessing in the dream of the ladder to heaven some twenty years before, Jacob now encounters God very personally, as he wrestles with a spiritual agony throughout the night until he finds peace in the knowledge of God's acceptance of him and the years of penance he has given. He has learnt so much during the years of working for Laban, and his perseverance and dedication have brought him to this point of full 'conversion' characterised by the new name he is given.

I CORINTHIANS 9:19-END

People today are highly aware of what they consider to be their 'rights'. Righteous indignation inflates every issue where our rights are threatened or violated, and sometimes we are so concerned with protecting our rights that we fail to remember our privileges.

Paul is not in the least concerned with his rights; he is more than willing to sacrifice them all if it means getting more souls for Christ. We may not live under the Mosaic

Law any more but we do live under God's law of love; and that can often cut clean across the worldly view of rights. Our unselfish caring, our willingness to forgive completely, our self discipline (all of which should be hallmarks of our life in Christ) may often be regarded as weakness and foolishness by a world which is obsessed by what it can gain rather than what it can give. And we are required, as part of our allegiance to Christ, to work for the spread of his kingdom using his methods. They are, in the end, the only methods which work.

MATTHEW 7:13-27

Since the man who built on sand is called 'foolish', we can assume that he had the choice of rock for his site, but for some reason decided against it. Perhaps the sand involved less work, and would provide quicker results. Both as individuals and in society and the Church we are often guilty of similar short-sightedness, and pay for it later.

Spiritually, we are particularly loath to dig deep foundations into hard rock, since it is painful and humiliating. And the house will look just as impressive from the surface whatever it is built on. Through history 'Christians' have been notorious for this: singing hymns while slaves died below decks; using their faith as an excuse to wage war and plunder; using their status as respectable people to lead self-indulgent or cruel lives. The whole body of the Church is weakened by the shame and sadness of such hypocrisy.

Tragically, many fine, sensitive people, and many longing for faith, have rejected Christ because of our pathetic building on sand. Jesus offers us strong rock on which to build lasting houses; lives built on Christ work – for the good of the whole world.

21st Sunday after Pentecost

Our Christian hope. As adopted children of God, we know that this world and this life is not the whole story. We are children of eternity, living in the faith that this life does not finish at death, and our true spiritual home is in heaven, towards which we are walking as joyful pilgrims.

YEAR 1

HABAKKUK 2:1-4

Habakkuk sees apparent injustice all around him. Evil often appears to be rewarded rather than punished, and it seems as if God's plans and promises are not being fulfilled. He lays these questions and doubts before God, and receives the assurance that God is indeed in control, even when our limited vision cannot see how things can possibly work out.

We need not worry about staging our own retribution or attempting to do God's planning for him. His timing is best, and we can rest assured that in God's good time all things will be fully accomplished in the way which is best and in accordance with God's nature of merciful love.

ACTS 26:1-8

Having been accused by the Jews of preaching against God, Paul couches his defence in terms which the Jews, and Agrippa, will recognise. He speaks of his hope as being the hope of all Jews – the hope foretold by all the prophets – of a time when all God's people would worship with God's chosen one, Messiah, among them. They would be the nucleus of light which would spread out to give light to the world.

The point of difference is that Paul claims Jesus to be the fulfilment of that hope, proved by God raising him to life after death, and thus opening to us all the chance of being raised to eternal life.

LUKE 18:1-8

The need for persistent prayer is illustrated here by Jesus in his story of the widow nagging a judge to give her justice. The judge is a thoroughly unsympathetic man, who would never help her but for her persistence, which finally drives him to act on her behalf. Jesus couldn't have chosen anyone less likely to grant a request, and yet in the end, justice is done. The contrast between this miserable judge and the all-loving God highlights the certainty of God being prepared to listen to us and see justice done. However long it takes we need never worry that God will turn down our request – it may well be that we are being taught perseverance and gaining a deeper faith in the process.

YEAR 2

EZEKIEL 12:21-END

If you have ever watched time-lapse photography in action you will have appreciated the wonder of how seemingly still things move, and plants grow. Much goes on imperceptibly under the earth during winter; we only see the glorious result burst out in the spring flowers. So it is with spiritual things: much growth happens during times we may be considering dead or unproductive times. Much later we may be able to look back and discern the painstaking development which has taken place, and of which the 'barren' section was necessary. God works all the time; he is working now; we can trust, even when we cannot see.

I PETER 1:13-21

Until Christ came to live among us in person we could not know God or hope and believe in him in quite the same way, because he had not yet been revealed to the world.

But Jesus changed all that, for in him we see the power and love of God acted out in human terms that we can understand.

Having acknowledged God as our Father, through seeing and listening to Jesus, we must be careful to act out our faith scrupulously as we journey through life to our heavenly home; not following meticulous rules of conduct, but living closely with Christ who will save us from evil.

JOHN 11:17-27
Mary, Martha and Lazarus had come to know God's love in person, through the time they had spent in Jesus' company.

When Lazarus dies, their faith in the living saviour is, as it were, brought to a head. This is the time when all their growth in spiritual understanding comes to flower. Martha recognises the power of Jesus' life-giving presence, and is convinced that if Jesus had been there her brother would still be alive. She is now led on by Jesus to see that he is not only the one who gives abundant life to his friends and followers – he is also life itself, divine as well as human, whose power of love is stronger even than death.

22nd Sunday after Pentecost

We cannot serve two masters – if we choose to serve God we shall not be able to continue as slaves of money and materialism. We should be as astute about our spiritual lives as the dishonest steward was about keeping his job.

YEARS 1 AND 2

DEUTERONOMY 11:18-28

We must never listen to the whisper of temptation which tells us we have done our choosing and our turning to God, and can sit back and relax. We may suddenly find that we have been worshipping all kinds of idols for quite some time.

We may find that some of our worst problems are actually the result of worshipping (or 'considering of great worth') the wrong things, and if we turn ourselves back to God, the problems may be solved or healed.

It is best to acknowledge our capacity for getting side-tracked, and set regular, thorough times for examining ourselves in the light of God's law of love. Then we can start to be reconciled with God before we have blundered too far in the opposite direction.

Moses well understands the way human memories are short and easily side-tracked. He knew from experience the initial bursts of enthusiasm gradually sinking into slackness. Few of us can keep going with sustained vigour for long; mostly we get distracted, and progress by lurching fitfully from resolution to resolution. That is why Moses suggests fastening the Law, quite literally, to our bodies, and the Law itself is a memory aid, useful for keeping us pointing in the right direction and turning us back if we have turned away.

I JOHN 2:22-END

John, too, urges us to keep the faith we hold alive. We need to run over it in our minds regularly: recite our faith together regularly, and then we will continue to live in Christ and he in us. This will also help to strengthen us against the temptation to rush off and get involved in the latest cult, in order, perhaps, to experience something emotional, rather than spiritual. This is certainly not suggesting stagnation. It is suggesting the anchor of true faith which will stop us drifting on strong currents which may look interesting but take us in the wrong direction.

LUKE 16:1-9

At first sight Jesus seems to be praising a steward for his dishonest behaviour. In fact he is comparing the shrewd, thorough way in which a dishonest man prepares for himself a settled future, with the vague uncommitted way we often go about preparing ourselves spiritually for our eternal future.

If we gave even a quarter as much attention to the development of our relationship with God as we give to the planning of a holiday, say, or the decorating scheme of the bathroom, we might start to really feel the effect of God's presence in our lives.

Suppose we prepared as carefully for communion as we do for arranging a dinner party for an important guest? Or spent as much time talking with God as we spend chatting to our friends at the pub or over a cup of tea?

Yet Jesus warns us that if we only use our time and energy pursuing money, material comforts and personal power, we shall not be serving God.

If, on the other hand, we regard all money and possessions as things to be used for good, and for God's glory, then our shrewd, wise handling of material goods may actually help us learn how to be responsible in spiritual matters.

Last Sunday after Pentecost

We are citizens of heaven, gradually making our way home. Before anything was created, and after the end of time, our God continues to reign. All who love him have been promised a share in his kingdom of heaven.

YEAR 1

JEREMIAH 29:1,4-14

God's word through Jeremiah to the exiled people of Israel is that they should contribute to the life of the community in which they find themselves, living caring lives to include the welfare of the Babylonians. They are to live in the present, in other words, doing good where they are, but at the same time looking forward to the time when they will be able to return to their own country.

In a way, this illustrates our own position: we are to live in this world to the full, but we are not to feel we belong to worldly values, since our home is the spiritual kingdom of heaven.

PHILIPPIANS 3:7-END

Paul has realised that his own efforts, however determined, will never be able to provide the lasting joy and peace which Christ offers, so nothing else is worth striving for.

Although living for Christ may well mean physical and spiritual hardship – even agony – it is worth every drop of suffering because the reward is so great. And the closer we get to being Christ-like, the more joy we shall find, and the more thankful we shall become.

JOHN 17:1-10

As Jesus nears the end of his saving work on earth, he prays for all his followers – us included – for whom he feels such love and for whom he is willing to undergo all the suffering of the cross.

When Jesus wrestles with burdens and problems he never does it alone. Always we read of his many hours of prayer in a solitary place where he could communicate with his heavenly Father. All his ministry was under-girded with the strength of this prayerfulness.

If we find ourselves having sleepless nights worrying about something, we ought to follow Jesus' example and worry it through with God instead of keeping it to ourselves. The difference is amazing. Instead of going round and round in circles with no glimpse of a solution anywhere, the whole process becomes manageable and productive. We may still spend sleepless hours thinking, but they are no longer chaotic and tense. Solutions may spring to mind which we had not even considered. (God, after all, can see the whole picture, not just the little section our human eyes are aware of.)

YEAR 2

ISAIAH 33:17-22
Living in turbulent times, with human weakness glaringly obvious, the prophet is led to see this vision of a different kind of rule in a kingdom of God's making.

Under such a reign there is justice blended with mercy, purity, and integrity. God is personally involved with his people and will care for them in an atmosphere of order, tranquillity and mutual respect.

The kingdom of heaven, later described so often by Jesus, is the fulfilment of such a vision, and directs us to a quality of life which will even continue beyond death.

REVELATION 7:2-4, 9-END
In this vision of heaven, the seer senses the awesome majesty and glorious beauty of everlasting life, suffused with purity and light. There, where there is no trace of sin any more, the fragments of perfection we have glimpsed throughout our

lives are concentrated in immeasurable, unlimited joy and worship and praise.

There we see, with a thrill of excitement, the countless numbers of faithful people from all over the world, and from every nation, pouring into the courts of heaven, to share its joy for ever.

MATTHEW 25:1-13

As we have seen, the early Christians expected Jesus to come in a matter of weeks or months, He did not, and here we are, nearly 2,000 years later, still waiting.

So this story of long waiting, yet still being prepared, is very useful. There is no doubt in the bridesmaids' minds about whether the bridegroom would come or not, and they had all brought their burning lamps with them. The only difference is that the five sensible ones had an extra oil supply with them so that their lamps would not go out after the initial burst of enthusiastic preparations.

We do need to refuel regularly if we are to stay 'alight', alert and ready to welcome Jesus. But we must do it ourselves – it is no good resting on other people's prayer lives, good works or depth of commitment to worship and care. Just because we are all members of the Church does not mean that we can jog casually along, not getting too involved while others dedicate their lives to serving Christ. If we do this, we shall find that our lamps are out when we need them most, and no borrowing of beautiful lives is possible.

In other words, how we live every second and every day determines how bright our lamps will be. Seconds may not seem very important, but life in Christ is painstakingly built, piece by piece, and a few grand gestures followed by months or years of complacency will not enable us to be made new in Christ. If we treasure each moment as an opportunity to refuel, then, when we meet him face to face, he will welcome us with joy.